50 Best
Stuffings
&
Dressings

Rick Rodgers

A John Boswell Associates/King Hill Productions Book
B r o a d w a y   B o o k s / N e w   Y o r k

BROADWAY

Broadway Books titles may be purchased for business or promotional use or for special sales. For information, please write to: Special Markets Department, Bantam Doubleday Dell Publishing Group, Inc., 1540 Broadway, New York, NY 10036.

Broadway Books and its logo, a letter B bisected on the diagonal, are trademarks of Broadway Books, a division of Bantam Doubleday Dell Publishing Group, Inc.

Library of Congress Cataloging-in-Publication Data

First Edition

Illustration and design by Richard Oriolo

ISBN 0-7679-0044-8

99 00 01 10 9 8 7 6 5 4 3

Contents

Introduction / 1

How to Make the Best Stuffing Ever / 3

Bread Stuffings / 11

Cornbread Stuffings / 31

Rice and Grain Stuffings / 49

Fruit and Vegetable Stuffings / 69

Meat Stuffings / 83

Index / 103

Introduction

Ask anyone what their favorite part of any holiday meal is, and chances are—it's the stuffing. Keeping this in mind, the question of what type of stuffing to make is no small matter, especially during the holidays, when you are making it to dress up a turkey or other large bird. Should it be a traditional bread stuffing seasoned with sausage and herbs, a cornbread stuffing spicy with the flavors of the Louisiana bayou, or a Spanish-inspired stuffing, loaded with pork, prunes, and chestnuts? What about including apples or bacon, potatoes or mushrooms, cranberries or nuts? Or perhaps oysters?

Most stuffings are based upon a starch of some kind—bread of all varieties (white bread and cornbread, of course, but also wheat, sourdough, and rye), potatoes, rice of many colors, or even grains, such as kasha. Many dressings play down the bread or omit it entirely to feature meats, nuts, vegetables, fruits, and other ingredients. In truth, I am never able to decide on just one recipe and have gotten into the habit on special occasions of making at least two stuffings, a custom in many homes, where the first stuffing is usually a traditional recipe that's been in the family for generations and the second one is something new every year.

Another decision about stuffing is what to call it? Most people who live in the South call it "dressing," while northerners call it "stuffing." Some argue that if it is cooked inside of the bird, it is a stuffing; cooked outside of the bird, it is a dressing. When something tastes so good, who cares what you call it?!

50 Best Stuffings and Dressings emphasizes stuffed turkey, because it is when roasting a big bird that most cooks are looking for innovations, inspiration, and guidance. Because a beautiful stuffed turkey is a traditional and sumptuous way to feed a crowd, it is always welcome on the holiday table, be it Thanksgiving or New Year's Day, Christmas or Passover. Almost all of these recipes, which can be baked in the bird or alongside, will work as well in a roaster chicken or capon. Any extra stuffing goes into a casserole to be baked while the roast turkey is standing before being carved.

I have also included a couple of recipes for that Easter dinner favorite, leg of lamb. Many of the recipes are versatile and can be adapted easily to other favorite stuffed foods, like duck, goose, chicken, Cornish hens, pork chops, crown roast of pork, zucchini, cabbage, eggplant, and sweet peppers.

How to Make the Best
Stuffing
Ever

Because I teach cooking and my most popular class offers a Thanksgiving menu, every year I make stuffed turkey about twenty times in a six-week period. That makes me pretty confident about sharing my secrets for the best stuffing you've ever poured gravy over. Following, along with tips to make your stuffing the tastiest and most successful ever, are recipes for the perfect roast turkey and foolproof gravy.

When planning your menu, allow ¾ to 1 cup of stuffing per serving, keeping in mind the appetites of your guests and family and allowing extra for seconds and leftovers. Most stuffing recipes can easily be divided or multiplied to make an amount that fits your needs.

A turkey can hold about ¾ cup of stuffing per pound. Loosely stuff the turkey in the large body cavity, as the dressing will expand as it cooks. Don't forget to put some stuffing in the neck pocket, too.   Since all the stuffing rarely fits inside a bird, put any leftovers in a lightly buttered casserole, cover, and refrigerate until ready to bake. As the stuffing won't be basted by the turkey juices, moisten with a little extra broth before baking. You'll need about ½ cup of liquid (homemade turkey broth, canned reduced-sodium chicken broth, wine, or water) for an entire batch of stuffing; adjust the amount accordingly if you have less.

Cover the dish with foil and bake the stuffing in a 350°F. oven until it is heated to 165°F. when tested with a meat thermometer, about 30 minutes. If you like crusty stuffing, remove the foil during the last 15 minutes. Since a turkey has to stand for at least 20 to 30 minutes before carving to allow the juices to settle back into the meat, the extra stuffing can be baked during this rest period.

A goose will hold 6 to 8 cups of stuffing. Roasting chickens and ducks have relatively small body cavities that really won't hold more than 2 or 3 cups of stuffing; even capons will only take 3 to 4 cups. So plan to bake the remainder on the side.

Time-Saving Tips: The night before, prepare the components of the recipe— chop vegetables, toast nuts, cube bread, and so on; seal them separately in plastic bags and refrigerate if necessary. The bread should be left uncovered at room temperature, so it has time to dry out.

If you're in a hurry, substitute a packaged bread stuffing mix, such as Pepperidge Farm, for freshly cubed bread. A (1-pound) loaf of firm-textured bread, regardless of type, is equal to about 10 cups of bread cubes. Just use the cup measurements provided in the recipes. Because packaged stuffing croutons are crisp, you will need more liquid to moisten the stuffing than you would with home-dried cubes.

Safety Tips: Here are some commonsense rules for stuffing turkey:

- Always stuff a turkey just before roasting, never ahead of time. Harmful bacteria can develop inside the cavity if the stuffed bird isn't roasted right away.
- Do not make the stuffing the night before you're planning to serve. To kill all harmful bacteria, the stuffing must be cooked to 160° to 165°F. If it has been prepared ahead and refrigerated, chances are the ice-cold filling won't reach that temperature by the time the bird is done. If because of time pressures you must begin the night before, cook the ingredients, but refrigerate them separately and don't mix them together until the next day. Warm the cooked ingredients in a large nonstick skillet before adding to the bread cubes, so the stuffing isn't too cold when it goes into the bird.

- If the bird is done but the stuffing isn't hot enough, remove the turkey from the oven. Spoon the stuffing out of the cavity and place in a buttered casserole. Cover and bake in a 350°F. oven until the stuffing reaches 165°F.
- Don't try to save time by mixing uncooked vegetables or raw meat into the stuffing. It will suffer in taste and texture as well as being a safety risk.
- Remove all the stuffing from the turkey before serving and place it in a serving bowl. Do not let the turkey or stuffing stand out at room temperature for longer than 2 hours. Refrigerate any leftovers separately from the meat and use within 2 days. Reheat leftover stuffing thoroughly before serving.

Ingredients

Stuffing is only as good as the ingredients that go into it. A lot of different flavors and textures combine to make a good stuffing, so it's worth taking a little care to ensure that each component is at its best.

The Bread

For traditional bread stuffings, choose a loaf with a firm texture and close crumb, such as a high-quality white sandwich bread. Avoid spongy, fluffy breads. Italian bread with a soft crust also works well. Don't trim off crusts; they add texture and color. A serrated knife does the best job of cutting the bread into ½- to ¾-inch cubes.

Always cube the bread the night before and allow it to dry out on a baking sheet at room temperature before using for stuffing. Air-dried bread holds its shape better when moistened and will keep your stuffing from becoming a soggy mess. As an alternative, bake the bread cubes in a preheated 350°F. oven, stirring occasionally, until they are dry and crisp and the edges are lightly browned, about 20 to 30 minutes.

The Seasonings

To ensure freshness and that your stuffings taste as good as mine do, make your own seasoning blends. It's also practical, since you probably have all the spices and herbs on your shelf. As an added bonus, your seasoning blends will have much less salt than supermarket varieties. Store any leftover seasoning blends in small, tightly covered jars.

Homemade Poultry Seasoning: Combine 1 teaspoon each dried rosemary, dried crumbled sage, dried thyme leaves, dried marjoram, and celery salt, and ¼ teaspoon freshly ground pepper. Crush together, preferably in a mortar and pestle or in a mini-food processor.

Homemade Cajun Seasoning: Stir together 2 tablespoons sweet Hungarian paprika, 1 teaspoon each dried basil and dried thyme, ½ teaspoon each garlic powder, onion powder, and freshly ground pepper, and ⅛ teaspoon cayenne.

Toasted Nuts

Roasting enhances the flavor of most nuts, and it improves their texture, especially if they are going to be steamed in a moist stuffing. While some nuts are sold roasted, many are not.

To toast walnuts, pecans, almonds, pistachio nuts, or hazelnuts: Spread the nuts in a single layer on a baking sheet and bake in a preheated 350°F. oven, stirring occasionally, until they are fragrant and lightly browned, 7 to 10 minutes. Check often, because nuts can burn quickly.

To skin hazelnuts: Wrap the warm nuts in a kitchen towel and let stand for 20 minutes. Using the towel, rub the nuts between your hands to remove as much of the dark outer skins as possible—don't worry if you don't get every bit.

To roast chestnuts: Preheat the oven to 400°F. Using a small, sharp knife, cut a deep "X" in the flatter side of each chestnut. Place in a single layer on a baking sheet and bake until the outer skin is split and crisp, about 30 minutes.

They never all seem to be done at the same time, so work with the ones that are ready and continue roasting the others. Place the roasted chestnuts in a kitchen towel to keep them warm. Using a small, sharp knife, peel off both the tough outer and thin inner skins. To loosen the peels on stubborn, hard-to-peel chestnuts, return to the oven for an additional 5 to 10 minutes, or microwave on High for 1 minute.

Vacuum-packed peeled chestnuts are available in 15-ounce jars at specialty food stores. Each jar is equivalent to 1 pound of chestnuts, roasted and peeled. Canned chestnuts are also available, but the flavor of freshly roasted or vacuum-packed is superior.

The Turkey

What's the point of roasting a turkey unless there are some leftovers for sandwiches? To ensure at least some leftovers, allow about 1½ pounds of turkey per person. An 18-pound bird will serve about 12 people.

While a young hen no bigger than 12 pounds is convenient for a smaller gathering, there is, in fact, more meat per bone on a larger turkey. These days, thanks to modern animal husbandry, all turkeys—of any sex, age, and size—are equally tender, provided they are cooked properly.

Perfect Roast Turkey with Gravy

Makes about 12 servings

This is, unequivocally, the best way to roast a turkey with the least amount of hassle. For success, you do need one piece of equipment: a sturdy, shallow roasting pan and rack. (Inexpensive disposable aluminum foil roasting pans are too flimsy and are impossible to make gravy in. Old-fashioned covered turkey roasters are too lightweight and so deep that the bird steams rather than roasts.) One last tip: Use a fresh, all-natural bird that has not been injected with oils and artificial flavors.

> 1 (18-pound) fresh turkey, neck and giblets reserved
> 10 to 12 cups of your favorite stuffing
> 6 tablespoons unsalted butter, softened
> 1 teaspoon salt
> ¼ teaspoon freshly ground pepper
> About 8 cups Turkey Broth (recipe follows)
> ½ cup all-purpose flour
> 3 tablespoons bourbon, port, or dry sherry, optional

1. Preheat the oven to 325°F. Rinse the turkey inside and out with cold water and pat dry. Turn the turkey on its breast. Loosely fill the neck cavity with stuffing. Using a thin metal or wooden skewer, pin the turkey's neck skin to the back. Fold the turkey's wings akimbo behind the back or tie to the body with kitchen string. Loosely fill the large body cavity with stuffing. Place any remaining stuffing in a lightly buttered casserole, cover, and refrigerate to bake as a side dish. Place the drumsticks in the hock lock or tie together with kitchen string.

2. Place the turkey on a rack in a large flameproof roasting pan that is no deeper than 3 inches. Rub all over with the softened butter. Season with the salt and pepper. Tightly cover the breast area with aluminum foil. Pour 2 cups of turkey stock into the bottom of the pan.

3. Roast the turkey, basting all over every 30 minutes with the juices on the bottom of the pan (lift up the foil to reach the breast area), until a meat thermometer inserted in the meaty part of the thigh (but not touching a bone) reads 175° to 180°F. and the stuffing is at least 160° to 165°F., about 5 hours and 40 minutes. If anytime during roasting the drippings on the bottom of the pan threaten to burn, add 1 cup water. Remove the foil during the last hour to allow the skin to brown.

4. Transfer the turkey to a large serving platter and let it stand for at least 20 minutes before carving. Increase the oven temperature to 350°F. Drizzle ½ cup of turkey broth over the stuffing in the casserole, cover, and bake until heated through, about 30 minutes.

5. Meanwhile, pour the drippings from the roasting pan into a heatproof glass bowl or measuring cup. Let stand 5 minutes; then skim off and reserve the clear yellow fat that rises to the top. Add enough turkey broth to the skimmed drippings to make 6 cups total.

6. Place the roasting pan over two stove burners on medium heat and add ½ cup of the reserved turkey fat. Whisk in the flour, scraping up the browned bits on the bottom of the pan, and cook until lightly browned, about 2 minutes. Whisk in the turkey broth and bourbon. Cook, whisking often, until the gravy has thickened and no trace of raw flour flavor remains, about 5 minutes. Transfer the gravy to a warmed gravy boat. Carve the turkey and serve the gravy alongside.

Note: Different size birds have varying roasting times: Stuffed hen turkeys (8 to 15 pounds) take about 20 minutes per pound; the larger toms (15 pounds and up) take about 15 minutes per pound. If you are roasting an unstuffed bird, delete about 3 minutes per pound from the estimated roasting times.

Turkey Broth: Using a heavy cleaver, chop 2 pounds turkey wings into 2-inch pieces (or ask the butcher to chop them). In a large flameproof casserole, heat 2 tablespoons vegetable oil. Add the giblets reserved from the turkey. Cook, stirring, over medium-high heat until browned, 5 to 7 minutes. Remove them with a slotted spoon and set aside. In batches, add the chopped turkey wings to the pot, adding more oil if needed, and cook, turning occasionally, until browned, 8 to 10 minutes per batch. Return the giblets and all the wings to the pan. Add 1 onion,

1 carrot, and 1 celery rib with leaves, all coarsely chopped. Add 3 quarts water, or enough to cover the ingredients by at least 2 inches. Bring to a boil, skimming off all the foam that rises to the top. Reduce the heat to low and add ½ teaspoon dried thyme leaves, 4 parsley sprigs, ¼ teaspoon black peppercorns, and 1 bay leaf. Simmer uncovered 2 to 3 hours. Strain the broth and let cool; skim all the fat from the top before using. **Makes about 8 cups**

Bread
Stuffings

If this cookbook were an art gallery, these recipes would be the Norman Rockwells—classic renditions that evoke nostalgia and warm feelings. For picture-perfect stuffings, remember these important tips:

- Use cubed bread that has dried overnight at room temperature or has been lightly toasted in the oven.
- The bread's dryness and texture will affect the amount of liquid needed to moisten the stuffing, so be flexible.
- In general, when chopping vegetables for stuffing, don't make them so small that they get lost. Keep the size relative to that of the bread cubes.
- Cook all ingredients that require cooking thoroughly before mixing into the stuffing. Don't try to save time by using raw vegetables or meat. Not only is it unsafe to use uncooked meat, but the raw vegetables will give the stuffing a very strong and unpleasant flavor after long cooking. Remember that the stuffing will only be warmed up, not actually cooked.
- Homemade turkey broth (page 9) makes the most flavorful stuffing, or use canned reduced-sodium chicken broth.

Classic Bread Stuffing with Onions, Celery, and Herbs

Makes about 10 cups

This classic American turkey stuffing is good as it stands, but it can also form the foundation for three other very popular variations—Giblet Stuffing, Oyster Stuffing, and Sausage Stuffing. My secret is a generous amount of celery leaves, which add a subtle, but distinctive difference. If you like your stuffing bound a little tighter with eggs, substitute 2 beaten eggs for ½ cup of the broth.

8 tablespoons (1 stick) unsalted butter

2 medium onions, chopped

3 medium celery ribs, chopped

½ cup chopped celery leaves (from inner celery ribs)

1 pound firm white sandwich bread, cut into ½-inch cubes and dried
      overnight or in the oven, or 10 cups plain bread croutons

¼ cup chopped fresh parsley

2 teaspoons poultry seasoning, preferably homemade (page 6)

1½ teaspoons salt

½ teaspoon freshly ground pepper

1½ to 2 cups turkey or chicken broth, as needed

1. In a large skillet, melt the butter over medium heat. Add the onions, celery, and celery leaves. Cook, stirring often, until the onions are golden, about 8 minutes.

2. Scrape the vegetables and butter into a large bowl. Mix in the bread cubes, parsley, poultry seasoning, salt, and pepper. Gradually stir in about 1½ cups of broth, until the stuffing is evenly moistened but not soggy. Use as a stuffing. Or place in a lightly buttered casserole, drizzle with ½ cup broth, cover, and bake as a side dish.

Giblet and Bread Stuffing: Use the giblets from your turkey. With a heavy cleaver, chop the turkey neck into 2- to 3-inch pieces. Trim the liver and refrigerate. In a large saucepan, cook the neck, heart, and gizzard in 1 tablespoon vegetable oil over medium-high heat, turning, until browned, about 10 minutes. Add 1 each quartered small onion and carrot, 3 parsley sprigs, and ¼ teaspoon thyme. Pour in enough chicken broth or water to cover by 1 inch. Bring to a simmer, skimming off any foam. Reduce the heat to low, partially cover, and simmer until the giblets are tender, about 1½ hours. Add the turkey liver and simmer until cooked through, 15 to 20 minutes. Strain, saving the stock if desired. Let the giblets cool. Pull the meat off the neck. Chop the neck meat, heart, gizzard, and liver. Stir into Classic Bread Stuffing (above) along with the bread cubes.

Oyster and Bread Stuffing: Drain 2 (8-ounce) containers of oysters and reserve the juices. (Or shuck 24 oysters, opening them over a fine wire sieve placed over a bowl to catch the juices.) If the oysters are large, cut them into 2 or 3 pieces. Add the oysters to Classic Bread Stuffing along with the bread cubes. Add enough turkey or chicken broth to the reserved oyster juices to make 1½ cups and use to moisten the stuffing mixture.

Sausage and Bread Stuffing: In a large skillet over medium heat, cook 1 pound bulk pork breakfast sausage, breaking up the meat with a spoon, until cooked through, about 10 minutes. Add to Classic Bread Stuffing (above) with the bread cubes and mix. Reduce the salt to 1 teaspoon.

Ham, Fennel, and Raisin Bread Stuffing

Makes about 12 cups

*C*ountry-style raisin bread is a great match for the flavors of fennel and smoked ham. Fresh fennel has a celery-like texture and an anise taste that works beautifully in turkey or chicken stuffings or to accompany roast pork. If your bakery has plain crusty country bread, but with no raisins in it, just add 1 cup of raisins.

8 tablespoons (1 stick) unsalted butter

1 large onion, chopped

1 medium bulb of fennel (¾ pound), cut into ¼-inch dice, plus ¼ cup
    chopped feathery tops, if included

½ pound smoked ham, chopped

¾ cup Madeira wine

1 teaspoon dried rosemary

1 pound crusty country-style raisin bread, cut into ½-inch cubes, dried
    overnight or in the oven (about 10 cups)

½ cup freshly grated Parmesan cheese

2 eggs, beaten

1 to 1½ cups turkey or chicken broth, as needed

½ teaspoon salt

¼ teaspoon freshly ground pepper

1. In a large skillet, melt the butter over medium heat. Add the onion and diced fennel, cover, and cook, stirring often, until the fennel is crisp-tender, about 10 minutes. Stir in the ham, Madeira, and rosemary. Bring to a boil.

2. Scrape the ham and fennel mixture into a large bowl. Add the bread cubes, Parmesan cheese, eggs, and chopped fennel tops and mix well. Gradually stir in about 1 cup broth, until the stuffing is evenly moistened but not soggy. Season with the salt and pepper. Use as a stuffing. Or place in a lightly buttered casserole, drizzle with ½ cup broth, cover, and bake as a side dish.

Quick Sausage, Apple, and Sage Stuffing

Makes about 8 cups

Sausage, apples, and sage are a classic New England stuffing trio, which lend fine flavor to turkey, chicken, and pork. Here dried apples are used to save time and add more concentrated flavor. They also tend to hold their shape and prevent the stuffing from becoming too wet.

1 tablespoon vegetable oil
1 large onion, finely chopped
3 medium celery ribs with leaves, finely chopped
1 pound bulk pork breakfast sausage
1 (16-ounce) package seasoned bread stuffing mix (8 cups)
1 cup packed coarsely chopped dried apples (3 ounces)
4 tablespoons unsalted butter, melted
¼ cup chopped fresh parsley
1 tablespoon chopped fresh sage or 1½ teaspoons crumbled dried
1½ to 2 cups turkey or chicken broth, as needed
Salt and freshly ground pepper

I. In a large skillet, heat the oil over medium heat. Add the onion and celery. Cook uncovered, stirring often, until the vegetables are softened, about 3 minutes. Add the sausage and cook, stirring often to break up the sausage with a spoon, until the sausage is cooked through, about 10 minutes.

2. Scrape the sausage mixture into a large bowl. Add the stuffing mix, dried apples, melted butter, parsley, and sage. Toss, gradually adding about 1½ cups broth, until the stuffing is evenly moistened but not soggy. Season with salt and pepper to taste. Use as a stuffing. Or place in a lightly buttered casserole, drizzle with ½ cup broth, cover, and bake as a side dish.

Whole Wheat Bread and Roasted Vegetable Stuffing

Makes about 8 cups

Roasting enhances the sweetness and deep flavor of autumn root vegetables. To save time, roast the vegetables the night before you make the stuffing. Don't be afraid to let the vegetables get nicely browned—the caramelization will only enhance their taste. Use with turkey, chicken, or pork.

3 tablespoons olive oil

3 large carrots, peeled and cut into ½-inch-thick rounds

2 large parsnips, peeled and cut into ½-inch-thick rounds

1 large celery root (1¼ pounds), peeled and cut into ½-inch cubes

1 large onion, cut into 6 wedges

1½ teaspoons salt

½ teaspoon freshly ground pepper

1 pound firm whole wheat or whole grain bread, cut into ½-inch cubes, dried overnight or in the oven (about 10 cups)

2 eggs, beaten

⅓ cup chopped fresh parsley

2 teaspoons poultry seasoning, preferably homemade (page 6)

1 to 1½ cups turkey or chicken broth, as needed

1. Preheat the oven to 450°F. In a large roasting pan, drizzle the oil over the carrots, parsnips, celery root, and onion and mix with your hands to coat the vegetables with the oil. Season with ½ teaspoon of the salt and ¼ teaspoon of the pepper. Roast, stirring the vegetables often, until they are tender and nicely browned, 35 to 45 minutes. Transfer to a bowl and let cool. On a work surface, coarsely chop the vegetables. (The roasted vegetables can be prepared up to 1 day ahead, covered, and refrigerated. Warm in a large nonstick skillet before using.)

2. Transfer the roasted vegetables to a large bowl. Mix in the bread cubes, eggs, parsley, poultry seasoning, and remaining 1 teaspoon salt and ¼ teaspoon pepper. Gradually stir in about 1 cup broth, until the stuffing is evenly moistened but not soggy. Or place in a lightly buttered casserole, drizzle with ½ cup broth, cover, and bake as a side dish.

Low-Fat Turkey Sausage and
Vegetable Stuffing

Makes about 14 cups

*F*or those who must watch their fat grams and calories for health reasons, here is a light, tasty turkey stuffing, enlivened with lean turkey sausage and bound with egg substitute.

Nonstick vegetable oil spray
1 medium onion, chopped
2 medium celery ribs with leaves, chopped
2 medium carrots, thinly sliced into rounds
2 garlic cloves, minced
1½ to 2 cups turkey or chicken broth, as needed
1 pound sweet Italian turkey sausage, casing removed
1 tablespoon poultry seasoning, preferably homemade (page 6)
½ teaspoon salt
¼ teaspoon freshly ground pepper
1 pound firm whole wheat or white sandwich bread (or a combination),
     cut into ½-inch cubes and dried overnight or in the oven (about 10 cups)
½ cup chopped fresh parsley
½ cup liquid egg substitute

1. Spray a large nonstick skillet with vegetable oil spray and place over medium heat. Add the onion, celery, carrots, and garlic. Add ½ cup of broth and bring to a boil. Cook, partially covered, stirring occasionally, until the broth has evaporated, about 10 minutes.

2. Add the turkey sausage and cook, stirring often and breaking up the meat with a spoon, until the sausage is cooked through, about 10 minutes. Stir in the poultry seasoning, salt, and pepper.

3. Scrape the sausage mixture into a large bowl. Mix in the bread cubes and parsley. Gradually stir in the liquid egg substitute and about 1 cup broth, until the stuffing is evenly moistened but not soggy. Use as a stuffing. Or place in a lightly buttered casserole, drizzle with ½ cup broth, cover, and bake as a side dish.

Sourdough Bread Stuffing with Artichokes, Sun-Dried Tomatoes, and Basil

Makes about 8 cups

If the Thanksgiving weather forecast is cold and gray, then you might want to consider this brightly colored stuffing, which is packed with sunny Mediterranean flavors and goes well with a variety of foods: turkey, chicken, pork, bell peppers, and zucchini. Don't cut the crusts off the bread; they add texture.

2 tablespoons olive oil

1 large red onion, chopped

2 garlic cloves, minced

1 (10-ounce) package frozen artichoke hearts, thawed and coarsely chopped

½ cup chopped sun-dried tomatoes in oil, drained

1 pound crusty sourdough bread, cut into ½-inch cubes and dried overnight or in the oven (about 10 cups)

½ cup chopped fresh basil

½ cup freshly grated Parmesan cheese

½ teaspoon salt

¼ to ½ teaspoon crushed hot red pepper, to taste

½ cup dry vermouth or white wine

2 eggs, beaten

1 cup turkey or chicken broth, as needed

1. In a large skillet, heat the olive oil over medium heat. Add the red onion and cook, stirring often, until lightly browned, about 6 minutes. Stir in the garlic and cook for 1 minute. Add the artichoke hearts and chopped sun-dried tomatoes and cook until heated through, about 2 minutes.

2. Scrape the vegetables into a large bowl. Add the bread cubes, basil, Parmesan cheese, salt, and hot pepper. Gradually stir in the vermouth, eggs, and about ½ cup broth, until the stuffing is evenly moistened but not soggy. Use as a stuffing. Or place in a lightly buttered casserole, drizzle with ½ cup broth, cover, and bake as a side dish.

Rick's Deluxe Turkey Stuffing

Sometimes when Thanksgiving rolls around, I just can't decide what kind of stuffing to make. So I cook up a little bit of everything, toss it all into a bowl, and stir. My guests love it, especially those who hold to the rule that the more "stuff" stuffing has in it, the better it is. This makes a big batch, more than enough for any size turkey and a casserole to bake on the side.

12 tablespoons (1½ sticks) unsalted butter

2 large onions, chopped

5 celery ribs with leaves, chopped

3 medium carrots, peeled and chopped

2 Granny Smith apples, peeled, cored, and chopped

4 garlic cloves, minced

2 tablespoons poultry seasoning, preferably homemade (page 6)

1 pound small mushrooms, quartered

1 cup dry white wine

2 pounds bulk pork breakfast sausage

1 (1-pound) bag seasoned bread stuffing mix (8 cups)

1 (1-pound) bag seasoned cornbread stuffing mix (8 cups)

2 pounds chestnuts, roasted and peeled (page 6), coarsely chopped

1 cup chopped fresh parsley

4 eggs, beaten

2 to 2½ cups turkey or chicken broth, as needed

1 teaspoon salt

½ teaspoon freshly ground pepper

1. In a large skillet, melt 1 stick of butter over medium heat. Add the onions, celery, carrots, apples, and garlic. Cover and cook, stirring often, until the carrots are crisp-tender, about 7 minutes. Increase the heat to medium-high. Uncover and cook, stirring often, until the onions are golden, about 10 minutes. Stir in the poultry seasoning. Scrape the vegetable mixture and butter into a very large bowl.

2. Add 2 tablespoons of butter to the skillet and melt over medium heat. Add the mushrooms. Cover and cook until the mushrooms begin to give off their liquid, about 3 minutes. Uncover and cook, stirring often, until the liquid evaporates and the mushrooms begin to brown, about 8 minutes. Pour in the wine and bring to a boil. Add to the vegetables in the bowl.

3. In the same skillet, melt the remaining 2 tablespoons of butter. Add the sausage and cook, stirring often and breaking up the meat with a spoon, until the sausage is cooked through, about 10 minutes. Add to the bowl and mix well.

4. Stir in the bread stuffing mixes, roasted chestnuts, and parsley. Gradually stir in the eggs and about 2 cups broth, until the stuffing is evenly moistened but not soggy. Season with the salt and pepper. Use as a stuffing. Or place in a lightly buttered casserole, drizzle with ½ cup broth, cover, and bake as a side dish.

Potato, Bacon, and Rye Bread Stuffing

Makes about 10 cups

*T*his *flavor-packed stuffing has its roots in the hearty cuisine of Scandinavia, where rye is used to make the bread of choice (the grain is easier to grow in cold climates than wheat). Wonderful with turkey, this stuffing really feels at home when served with roast goose or duck, but a half recipe will probably be sufficient for these smaller birds.*

    1 pound sliced bacon
    3 pounds medium red or yellow potatoes, scrubbed
    ¼ cup bacon fat or vegetable oil
    3 celery ribs, chopped
    6 scallions, chopped
    1 tablespoon caraway seed
    1 pound rye bread, cut into ½-inch cubes and dried overnight or in
          the oven (about 10 cups)
    1 to 1½ cups turkey or chicken broth, as needed
    Salt and freshly ground pepper

1. Preheat the oven to 400°F. Place the bacon strips in a single layer on a large rimmed baking sheet or jelly-roll pan. Bake in the upper third of the oven until crisp and browned, 10 to 15 minutes. Some strips of bacon will cook more quickly than others, so remove them as they crisp and drain on paper towels. Crumble when cool. As the bacon fat renders and accumulates in the baking sheet, pour it off into a small heatproof bowl; reserve ¼ cup.

2. Place the potatoes in a large saucepan and add enough lightly salted cold water to cover by 2 inches. Bring to a boil over high heat. Cook until the potatoes are barely tender when pierced with a knife, 15 to 20 minutes. Drain, rinse under cold water, and cool until easy to handle. Cut into 1-inch cubes.

3. In a large skillet, heat the reserved bacon fat or the oil over medium heat. Add the celery and cook, stirring often, until softened, about 5 minutes. Add the scallions and caraway seed. Cook, stirring occasionally, until the celery is beginning to brown, about 5 more minutes.

4. Scrape the celery mixture into a large bowl. Add the bread cubes, cubed potatoes, and crumbled bacon. Toss to mix. Gradually stir in about 1 cup broth until the stuffing is evenly moistened but not soggy. Season with salt and pepper to taste. Use as a stuffing. Or place in a lightly buttered casserole, drizzle with ½ cup broth, cover, and bake as a side dish.

Peppery Sausage and Cracker Stuffing

Makes about 8 cups

*E*very family has its own stuffing traditions etched in stone: bread, rice, meat.... In some households, it's saltine crackers, whose inherent crispness makes them a prime stuffing candidate. This one works well in turkey or chicken.

2 tablespoons olive oil

1 large onion, chopped

2 medium celery ribs, chopped

1 small green bell pepper, chopped

1 small red bell pepper, chopped

2 garlic cloves, minced

1 pound hot Italian sausage, casings removed

2 teaspoons dried basil

2 teaspoons dried oregano

¾ pound (3 rows) unsalted saltine crackers, coarsely crushed

1 to 1½ cups turkey or chicken broth, as needed

2 eggs, beaten

½ teaspoon salt

¼ teaspoon freshly ground pepper

1. In a very large skillet or flameproof casserole, heat the oil over medium heat. Add the onion, celery, green pepper, red pepper, and garlic. Cook, stirring often, until the vegetables are softened, about 5 minutes.

2. Add the sausage. Increase the heat to medium-high. Cook, stirring often and breaking up the sausage with a spoon, until the sausage is cooked through, about 10 minutes. Stir in the basil and oregano. Remove from the heat.

3. Place the crackers in a large bowl and gradually stir in 1 cup of the broth. Scrape the sausage mixture into the bowl and mix. Stir in the eggs, salt, and pepper. If necessary, add a little more broth so the stuffing is evenly moistened but not soggy. Use as a stuffing. Or place in a lightly buttered casserole, drizzle with ½ cup broth, cover, and bake as a side dish.

New England Oyster and Corn Chowder Stuffing

Makes about 12 cups

Oyster stuffing is one of our oldest American culinary traditions, dating back to Pilgrim times. My favorite version for turkey or chicken uses the potatoes, bacon, and cream found in a Yankee oyster chowder. Oyster crackers, the kind for sprinkling on top of chowders, make a fine base for stuffing. Notice only a little salt is added, because the bacon, crackers, and oysters are all salty ingredients.

1 pound medium red potatoes, scrubbed

½ pound sliced bacon

1 large onion, chopped

3 celery ribs with leaves, chopped

1 medium red bell pepper, chopped

1 teaspoon dried thyme leaves

6 cups oyster crackers (12 ounces), coarsely crushed

2 cups fresh or thawed frozen corn kernels

⅓ cup chopped fresh parsley

2 cups heavy cream

2 (8-ounce) containers oysters, drained, with juices reserved (or 24 freshly
      shucked oysters with juices), large oysters cut into 2 or 3 pieces

2 eggs, beaten

½ to 1 cup turkey or chicken broth, as needed

½ teaspoon salt

½ teaspoon freshly ground pepper

1. In a medium saucepan of boiling salted water, cook the potatoes over medium-high heat until just tender, 15 to 20 minutes. Drain and rinse under cold running water. Peel the potatoes if you wish. Cut them into ½-inch cubes.

2. Meanwhile, in a large skillet, cook the bacon over medium heat, turning, until lightly browned and crisp, 8 to 10 minutes. Remove with tongs and drain the bacon on paper towels. Crumble when cool. Reserve the fat in the skillet.

3. Add the onion, celery, red pepper, and thyme to the bacon fat in the skillet. Cook, stirring often, until the onion is softened and beginning to color, about 8 minutes.

4. Scrape the vegetable mixture into a large bowl. Mix in the crackers, crumbled bacon, cooked potatoes, corn, and parsley. Gradually stir in the cream, reserved oyster juices, eggs, and about ½ cup broth, until the stuffing is evenly moistened but not soggy. Season with the salt and pepper. Let stand for 15 minutes, stirring occasionally, allowing the crackers to absorb the liquid. Add the oysters and mix gently. Use as a stuffing. Or place in a lightly buttered casserole, drizzle with ½ cup broth, cover, and bake as a side dish.

Pumpernickel and Rye Bread Stuffing with Apples, Walnuts, and Golden Raisins

Makes about 10 cups

Two kinds of bread used here give a nice tang to this extra-chunky turkey stuffing, loaded with nuts and raisins. It is also an excellent stuffing to halve and use to stuff goose or ducks.

8 tablespoons (1 stick) unsalted butter

1 large onion, chopped

3 Granny Smith apples, peeled, cored, and cut into ½-inch cubes

2 medium celery ribs, chopped

1½ cups walnuts, toasted (see page 6) and coarsely chopped

1 cup golden raisins

½ pound pumpernickel bread (not Westphalian-style), cut into ½-inch cubes and
    dried overnight or in the oven (about 5 cups)

½ pound rye bread, cut into ½-inch cubes and dried overnight or in the oven
    (about 5 cups)

½ cup apple cider

½ to 1 cup turkey or chicken broth, as needed

Salt and freshly ground pepper

1. In a large skillet, melt the butter over medium heat. Add the onion and cook, stirring often, until softened, about 3 minutes. Add the apples and celery and cook, stirring often, until the onions are golden brown, about 10 minutes. Stir in the walnuts and raisins.

2. Transfer the onion-apple mixture to a large bowl. Add the pumpernickel and rye bread cubes. Toss, sprinkling with the apple cider. Gradually stir in about ½ cup broth, until the stuffing is evenly moistened but not soggy. Season with salt and pepper to taste. Use as a stuffing. Or place in a lightly buttered casserole, sprinkle with ½ cup broth, cover, and bake as a side dish.

Cornbread
Stuffings

"If it's not cornbread, it's not dressing!" Those are pretty strong words, but they are not uncommon in the South, where everyone calls stuffing "dressing." While my family always served white bread stuffing, when I left the nest, I learned to love golden brown cornbread dressing. For my own Thanksgiving meals, when I make at least two stuffings, cornbread always makes it onto the menu.

The best cornbread stuffing is made from home-baked cornbread. My Old-Fashioned Cornbread, which is a good consistency for stuffing, follows on page 32. As long as it contains no sugar, almost any recipe will serve, but the cornbread must be dried thoroughly in the oven before mixing with the other ingredients. Sugar will ruin a savory stuffing, so leave it out. If baking cornbread from a boxed mix or buying it from a bakery, be sure it is unsweetened. For convenience, you can use packaged cornbread stuffing instead of freshly baked, but because it is crisp, the stuffing will need extra liquid for moistening.

Old-Fashioned Cornbread for Stuffing

To save time, I bake this cornbread batter in a jelly-roll pan; it yields a thinner bread that is easier to crumble and dry out. The bread can also be baked in a 9 by 13-inch baking pan for about 25 minutes. (To make 5 cups crumbled cornbread, use half of the ingredients, pour into a buttered 8-inch square baking pan, and bake for about 20 minutes.)

2½ cups yellow cornmeal, preferably stone-ground

1½ cups all-purpose flour

4 teaspoons baking soda

1 teaspoon salt

2 cups milk

6 tablespoons unsalted butter, melted

2 eggs, beaten

1. Preheat the oven to 375°F. Lightly butter an 11 by 17 by 1-inch jelly-roll pan.

2. In a large bowl, whisk the cornmeal, flour, baking soda, and salt to combine. Make a well in the center and pour in the milk, butter, and eggs. Stir just until smooth. Transfer to the prepared pan and smooth the top with a metal spatula.

3. Bake until the top is golden brown and springs back when gently pressed in the center, about 20 minutes. Let cool in the pan on a wire cake rack. (The cornbread can be prepared up to 1 day ahead, covered, and stored at room temperature, or wrapped in aluminum foil and frozen for up to 1 month.)

4. To use for stuffing, crumble the cornbread right into the jelly-roll pan. Let stand overnight at room temperature to dry out, or toast lightly in a 350°F. oven for 15 to 20 minutes.

Greens and Bacon Cornbread Stuffing

Makes about 10 cups

Here's a unique Southern stuffing that goes well with either turkey or pork.

½ pound sliced bacon

2 medium turnips (¾ pound), peeled and cut into ½-inch cubes

1 medium onion, chopped

2 garlic cloves, minced

1 tablespoon Cajun seasoning, preferably homemade (page 6)

10 cups coarsely crumbled Old-Fashioned Cornbread (page 32), dried overnight or in the oven, or packaged cornbread stuffing

1 (1-pound) package frozen chopped collard greens, thawed and squeezed well to remove excess moisture

2 eggs, beaten

½ to 1 cup turkey or chicken broth, as needed

½ teaspoon salt

¼ teaspoon freshly ground pepper

1. In a skillet, cook the bacon over medium heat, until lightly browned and crisp, 8 to 10 minutes. Remove the bacon and drain on paper towels; crumble when cool. Pour off all but ¼ cup of the fat from the skillet.

2. Add the turnips to the fat in the skillet. Cook over medium heat, stirring occasionally, until lightly browned, about 5 minutes. Add the onion and cook until golden brown, about 8 minutes. Stir in the garlic and cook for 1 minute. Stir in the Cajun seasoning.

3. Scrape into a large bowl. Add the cornbread, crumbled bacon, and collard greens. Mix well. Gradually stir in the eggs and about ½ cup broth, until the stuffing is evenly moistened but not soggy. Season with the salt and pepper. Use as a stuffing for turkey. Or place in a lightly buttered casserole, drizzle with ½ cup broth, cover, and bake as a side dish.

Quick Southern Cornbread Dressing with Ham, Peaches, and Peanuts

Makes about 8 cups

*U*sing *purchased seasoned cornbread croutons, this tasty stuffing for turkey, chicken, or pork can be put together quickly. The flavorful ham and dried peaches provide fine results with little effort. Note: If you omit the ham from the stuffing, it makes a good side dish for a baked ham.*

1½ cups dried peaches (½ pound), cut into ½-inch cubes

⅓ cup bourbon or apple juice

8 tablespoons (1 stick) unsalted butter

½ pound smoked or boiled ham, cut into ½-inch cubes

6 scallions, chopped

1 teaspoon poultry seasoning, preferably homemade (page 6)

1 (16-ounce) package seasoned cornbread stuffing (8 cups)

2 eggs, beaten

1 cup coarsely chopped unsalted dry-roasted peanuts

1 to 1½ cups turkey or chicken broth, as needed

¼ teaspoon salt

¼ teaspoon freshly ground pepper

1. Place the peaches and bourbon in a small saucepan. Bring to a simmer over low heat. Remove from the heat, cover, and let stand while preparing the rest of the stuffing.

2. In a large skillet, melt the butter over medium heat. Add the ham and scallions and cook until the scallions are softened, about 3 minutes. Stir in the peaches, bourbon, and poultry seasoning.

3. Scrape the ham mixture into a large bowl. Add the cornbread stuffing, the peaches with their bourbon, the eggs, and the peanuts. Blend well. Gradually stir in about 1 cup broth, until the stuffing is evenly moistened but not soggy. Season with the salt and pepper. Use as a stuffing. Or place in a lightly buttered casserole, drizzle with ½ cup broth, cover, and bake as a side dish.

Gingered Cranberry and Almond
Cornbread Stuffing

Makes about 12 cups

*T*angy fresh cranberries need to be cooked first in a light syrup to reduce their tartness before being added to stuffing. Stir a tablespoon of the drained cooking liquid from the cranberries into a glass of chilled white wine for a holiday cocktail. Remember this recipe when preparing stuffing for pork chops, a crown roast of pork, roast chicken, or turkey.

1 cup sugar

1 (12-ounce) bag fresh cranberries, rinsed and picked over

8 tablespoons (1 stick) unsalted butter

1 large onion, chopped

3 medium celery ribs with leaves, chopped

2 tablespoons shredded fresh ginger (shredded on the large holes of a cheese grater)

10 cups coarsely crumbled Old-Fashioned Cornbread (page 32), dried overnight or in the oven, or packaged cornbread stuffing

1 cup slivered blanched almonds, toasted and coarsely chopped

2 eggs, beaten

1 to 1½ cups turkey or chicken broth, as needed

1 teaspoon salt

½ teaspoon freshly ground pepper

1. In a medium saucepan, bring the sugar and 1 cup water to a boil over high heat, stirring often to dissolve the sugar. Boil for 3 minutes. Add the cranberries and cook until the skins split, about 3 minutes. Do not overcook; the cranberries should remain relatively whole. Drain them in a wire sieve.

2. In a large skillet, melt the butter over medium heat. Add the onion and celery and cook, stirring often, until the onion is golden, about 8 minutes. Add the ginger and stir for 1 minute.

3. Scrape the cooked vegetables into a large bowl. Add the cornbread, drained cranberries, and almonds. Gradually stir in the eggs and about 1 cup broth, until the stuffing is evenly moistened but not soggy. Season with the salt and pepper. Use as a stuffing. Or place in a lightly buttered casserole, drizzle with ½ cup broth, cover, and bake as a side dish.

Mason-Dixon Cornbread Dressing
with Bacon and Pecans

Richness and full flavor, two hallmarks of Southern cooking, make this stuffing a treat inside a turkey or roasting chicken or alongside a roast of pork.

1 pound sliced bacon

⅓ cup reserved bacon fat

2 medium onions, chopped

3 medium celery ribs with leaves, chopped

2 Granny Smith apples, peeled, cored, and chopped

1 medium green bell pepper, chopped

1 tablespoon poultry seasoning, preferably homemade (page 6)

10 cups coarsely crumbled Old-Fashioned Cornbread (page 32), dried overnight
     or in the oven, or packaged cornbread stuffing

1 cup pecans, toasted (see page 6) and coarsely chopped

⅓ cup chopped fresh parsley

1 cup half-and-half or light cream

2 eggs, beaten

¾ teaspoon salt

¼ teaspoon freshly ground pepper

½ cup turkey or chicken broth, optional

1. Preheat the oven to 400°F. Bake the bacon as directed in Step 1 on page 24. Reserve ⅓ cup of the fat. Drain the bacon; crumble when cool.

2. In a large skillet, heat the reserved bacon fat over medium heat. Add the onions, celery, apples, and green pepper. Cook, stirring often, until the onions are softened and translucent, about 10 minutes. Add the poultry seasoning and cook for 1 minute.

3. Scrape the vegetable mixture into a large bowl. Mix in the cornbread, crumbled bacon, pecans, and parsley. Gradually beat in the half-and-half and eggs. Season with the salt and pepper. Use as a stuffing. Or place in a lightly buttered casserole, drizzle with the broth, cover, and bake as a side dish.

Crab Gumbo Stuffing

Crab may be the best shellfish to use in stuffing, because you don't have to worry about overcooking it. This is one of my most popular stuffings, excellent in a turkey or chicken and tempting as well inside a large whole fish, such as snapper or bass, or sandwiched between two fish fillets.

8 tablespoons (1 stick) unsalted butter
1 pound andouille sausage or smoked pork or turkey kielbasa, cut into ½-inch
    cubes
1 large onion, chopped
6 scallions, chopped
3 celery ribs with leaves, chopped
1 medium red bell pepper, chopped
2 garlic cloves, minced
1 tablespoon Worcestershire sauce
1 tablespoon Cajun seasoning, preferably homemade (page 6)
10 cups coarsely crumbled Old-Fashioned Cornbread (page 32), dried overnight
    or in the oven, or packaged cornbread stuffing
1 pound crabmeat, picked over for cartilage
½ cup chopped fresh parsley
2 eggs, beaten
1 to 1½ cups turkey or chicken broth, as needed
½ teaspoon salt
¼ teaspoon freshly ground pepper

I. In a large skillet, melt the butter over medium-high heat. Add the sausage and cook, stirring often, until lightly browned, about 5 minutes. Using a large slotted spoon, transfer the sausage to a plate, leaving the fat in the skillet.

2. Add the onion, scallions, celery, red pepper, and garlic to the skillet. Cook over medium heat, stirring often, until the onion is softened and translucent, about 10 minutes. Stir in the Worcestershire sauce and Cajun seasoning until well mixed.

3. Scrape the cooked vegetables into a large bowl. Mix in the cornbread, cooked sausage, crabmeat, and parsley. Gradually stir in the eggs and about 1 cup broth, until the stuffing is evenly moistened but not soggy. Season with the salt and pepper. Use as a stuffing. Or place in a lightly buttered casserole, drizzle with ½ cup broth, cover, and bake as a side dish.

Dirty Cornbread Stuffing with Turkey Giblets

When a Southern cook calls a dish "dirty," it means it looks that way from being cooked with ground giblets and sausage. Giblet lovers will claim this turkey stuffing as a favorite. Pretty? Not really. Tasty? Yes!

1 pound andouille sausage or smoked pork or turkey kielbasa (see Note)

Turkey heart, gizzard (gristle removed), and liver, trimmed

6 tablespoons unsalted butter

2 medium onions, chopped

2 medium celery ribs, chopped

1 medium red bell pepper, chopped

2 garlic cloves, minced

1 tablespoon Cajun seasoning, preferably homemade (page 6)

10 cups coarsely crumbled Old-Fashioned Cornbread (page 32), dried
    overnight or in the oven, or packaged cornbread stuffing

⅓ cup chopped fresh parsley

2 eggs, beaten

1 to 1½ cups turkey or chicken broth, as needed

½ teaspoon salt

¼ teaspoon freshly ground pepper

1. Remove the casings from the sausage and cut into ½-inch-thick rounds. In a food processor, process the sausage, turkey heart, gizzard, and liver until finely ground.

2. In a large nonstick skillet, melt the butter over medium-high heat. Add the onions, celery, red pepper, and garlic. Cook, stirring often, until the onions are softened, about 4 minutes. Add the ground meat mixture. Cook, stirring often, until the meats are well cooked, about 10 minutes. Stir in the Cajun seasoning.

3. Scrape the meat mixture into a large bowl. Mix in the cornbread and parsley. Gradually stir in the eggs and about 1 cup broth, until the stuffing is evenly moistened but not soggy. Season with the salt and pepper. Use as a stuffing. Or place in a lightly buttered casserole, drizzle with ½ cup broth, cover, and bake as a side dish.

Note: 1 pound additional turkey (or chicken) giblets and livers, in any combination, can be substituted for the sausage.

Bayou Eggplant and Shrimp Stuffing

Makes about 14 cups

Inspired by an eggplant filled with cornbread and shrimp that I enjoyed once at a little restaurant near Breaux Bridge, Louisiana, this substantial stuffing lends itself well to either turkey or fish. Since eggplant soaks up oil like a sponge, I reduce the fat by using a large nonstick skillet.

3 tablespoons olive oil

1 large onion, chopped

2 medium celery ribs with leaves, chopped

1 medium red bell pepper, chopped

2 garlic cloves, minced

1 large eggplant (1½ pounds), cut into 1-inch cubes

1 pound medium shrimp, peeled, deveined, and coarsely chopped

1 tablespoon Cajun seasoning, preferably homemade (page 6)

10 cups coarsely crumbled Old-Fashioned Cornbread (page 32), dried
      overnight or in the oven, or packaged cornbread stuffing

⅓ cup chopped fresh parsley

3 eggs, beaten

1 to 1½ cups turkey or chicken broth, as needed

¾ teaspoon salt

¼ teaspoon freshly ground pepper

1. In a very large nonstick skillet, heat the oil over medium heat. Add the onion, celery, bell pepper, and garlic. Cover and cook, stirring occasionally, until the onion is softened, about 5 minutes. Stir in the eggplant. Cover and continue cooking, stirring often, until the eggplant is tender, 8 to 10 minutes.

2. Add the shrimp and Cajun seasoning. Cook, uncovered, stirring often, until the shrimp just turn pink and firm, 2 to 3 minutes.

3. Transfer the shrimp and vegetable mixture to a large bowl. Add the cornbread and parsley. Gradually stir in the eggs and about 1 cup broth, until the stuffing is evenly moistened but not soggy. Season with the salt and pepper. Use as a stuffing. Or place in a lightly buttered casserole, drizzle with ½ cup broth, cover, and bake as a side dish.

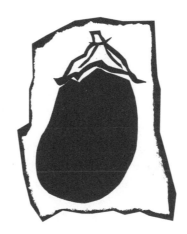

Portuguese Cornbread Stuffing with Clams and Spicy Sausage

Makes about 10 cups

Pork and clams, a favorite Portuguese combination, is similar in concept to some American favorites that combine pork and shellfish, such as gumbo and chowder. Cornbread is popular in Portugal, too, so this recipe is not a hybrid fantasy at all. Linguiça is a spicy, garlicky, smoked sausage similar to Spanish chorizo, but any spicy sausage will do. Use with turkey or pork.

¼ cup olive oil

1 pound linguiça, chorizo, or other spicy smoked sausage, cut into ½-inch cubes

2 medium onions, chopped

1 large red bell pepper, chopped

2 garlic cloves, minced

1 tablespoon ground cumin

1 tablespoon dried oregano

10 cups coarsely crumbled Old-Fashioned Cornbread (page 32), dried overnight or in the oven, or packaged cornbread stuffing

3 (8-ounce) cans chopped clams, with juices

2 eggs, beaten

½ cup chopped fresh cilantro

¾ to 1¼ cups turkey or chicken broth, as needed

½ teaspoon salt

¼ teaspoon freshly ground pepper

1. In a large skillet, heat the oil over medium-high heat. Add the sausage and cook, stirring often, until lightly browned, about 5 minutes. Using a large slotted spoon, transfer the sausage to a plate, leaving the fat in the skillet.

2. Add the onions and red pepper to the skillet. Cook over medium heat, stirring often, until the onions are softened and translucent, 3 to 5 minutes. Add the garlic, cumin, and oregano and stir for 30 seconds.

3. Scrape the cooked vegetables into a large bowl. Mix in the cornbread, reserved sausage, clams with their juices, eggs, and cilantro. Gradually stir in about ¾ cup broth, until the stuffing is evenly moistened but not soggy. Season with the salt and pepper. Use as a stuffing. Or place in a lightly buttered casserole, drizzle with ½ cup broth, cover, and bake as a side dish.

Rice and Grain
Stuffings

Besides being healthful and nutritious, most grains—and many types of rice—possess a mild nutty taste and sturdy texture that provide excellent foundations upon which to build a stuffing. Wild rice (although a grass, not a grain) has long held a top-ranking position in the stuffing hall of fame, but other rices and grains make worthwhile contributions, too.

The key is to not overcook the grain to begin with; keep in mind that the stuffing will be steamed for quite a while inside the bird. Boiling the grain in a large amount of salted water is a good way to control the texture. Cook it only until al dente, that is, until tender but still firm enough to feel a little chewy. Allow about fifteen minutes for long-grain white rice (including basmati), twenty minutes for converted rice, thirty-five minutes for brown rice, and forty-five minutes for wild rice. When cooking white rice for a stuffing, I tend to prefer the converted variety. Converted rice is steamed and dehydrated before packaging, which removes the surface starch, so it cooks up into separate grains that retain their shape better than the ordinary variety and stick together less. Many rices that are not converted—such as popcorn, wild pecan, and jasmine— are naturally fragrant, and it's fun to use them for variety.

Whole grains also offer a range of tastes and textures that can enhance stuffings. Cooked rye or wheat berries make an interesting substitute for brown or wild rice. Some grains, such as couscous, millet, and quinoa, are too delicate to stand up to long cooking, so if you use them in stuffings, bake them outside the bird.

Aromatic Basmati Rice with Apricots and Cashews

Makes about 11 cups

Gently spiced with fragrant Indian seasonings, this stuffing is a fine filling for chicken, duck, or Cornish game hens as well as turkey.

2½ cups (1 pound) basmati rice
4 tablespoons unsalted butter
2 medium onions, halved and sliced ½ inch thick
2 medium carrots, peeled and cut into ½-inch dice
1 teaspoon ground cardamom
1 teaspoon ground ginger
½ teaspoon ground cinnamon
½ teaspoon ground turmeric
¼ teaspoon ground cloves
1 cup roasted unsalted cashews (see Note), coarsely chopped
1 cup chopped dried apricots
⅓ cup chopped fresh cilantro or parsley
1½ teaspoons salt
½ teaspoon freshly ground pepper
½ cup turkey or chicken broth, optional

1. Bring a large pot of lightly salted water to a boil over high heat. Add the rice and reduce the heat to medium. Boil uncovered until the rice is barely tender, about 15 minutes. Drain into a sieve and rinse under cold running water. Place in a large bowl.

2. In a large skillet, melt the butter over medium-high heat. Add the onions and carrots. Cook, stirring often, until the onions are golden brown, 10 to 12 minutes. Add the cardamom, ginger, cinnamon, turmeric, and cloves and stir until very fragrant, 15 to 30 seconds.

3. Scrape the vegetables into the bowl of rice and mix. Stir in the cashews, apricots, cilantro, salt, and pepper. Use as a stuffing. Or place in a lightly buttered baking dish, drizzle with the broth, cover, and bake as a side dish.

Note: If you can't find unsalted roasted cashews, simply rinse the salted ones under cold running water and pat dry.

Chinese Hidden Treasure Stuffing

Makes about 12 cups

This mélange of many Asian ingredients usually finds its way into a boned duck, but it is equally delicious when stuffed in a turkey or capon. It is packed with hidden treasures like sweet chestnuts, crunchy water chestnuts, aromatic cilantro, and salty prosciutto, which is actually very similar to traditional Chinese dry-cured ham.

1 ounce dried black Chinese mushrooms (about 8 mushrooms)

2½ cups (1 pound) jasmine or Jasmati rice

2 tablespoons vegetable oil

4 scallions, chopped

3 celery ribs, finely chopped

¼ pound thickly sliced prosciutto or Smithfield ham, cut into ¼-inch dice

1 (8-ounce) can sliced water chestnuts, rinsed and coarsely chopped

1 (8-ounce) can sliced bamboo shoots, rinsed and coarsely chopped

3 tablespoons shredded fresh ginger

3 tablespoons dry sherry

3 tablespoons soy sauce

1 pound chestnuts, roasted and peeled, (page 7), coarsely chopped

½ cup chopped fresh cilantro

¾ teaspoon salt

¼ teaspoon freshly ground pepper

½ cup turkey or chicken broth, optional

1. Place the dried mushrooms in a small bowl and add enough boiling water to cover. Let stand until softened, 20 to 30 minutes. Drain the mushrooms. Cut off and discard the tough stems, and coarsely chop the caps. Set aside.

2. Bring a large pot of lightly salted water to a boil over high heat. Add the rice and reduce the heat to medium. Boil uncovered until the rice is barely tender, about 15 minutes. Drain and rinse under cold running water. Place in a large bowl.

3. In a large skillet or wok, heat the oil over medium-high heat. Add the scallions, celery, prosciutto, water chestnuts, bamboo shoots, ginger, sherry, and soy sauce. Stir-fry until the celery is crisp-tender, about 3 minutes.

4. Scrape the vegetable mixture into the bowl of rice. Mix in the roasted chestnuts and cilantro. Season with the salt and pepper. Use as a stuffing. Or place in a lightly buttered casserole, drizzle with the broth, cover, and bake as a side dish.

Jambalaya Ham and Oyster Stuffing

Makes about 9 cups

Zesty jambalaya, the rice dish of the Bayou, studded with ham and oysters, makes a terrific stuffing for turkey or side dish for roast pork or pork chops.

2½ cups (1 pound) converted white rice

8 tablespoons (1 stick) unsalted butter

½ pound smoked or boiled ham, cut into ½-inch dice

1 large onion, chopped

2 medium celery ribs with leaves, chopped

1 medium green bell pepper, chopped

4 scallions, chopped

2 garlic cloves, minced

1 tablespoon Cajun seasoning, preferably homemade (page 6)

1 (15-ounce) can tomato sauce

1 to 1½ cups turkey or chicken broth, as needed

1 tablespoon Worcestershire sauce

1 teaspoon salt

¼ teaspoon freshly ground black pepper

2 (8-ounce) containers oysters, drained, or 24 freshly shucked oysters, cut into
    2 or 3 pieces if large

1. Bring a large pot of lightly salted water to a boil over high heat. Add the rice and reduce the heat to medium. Boil until the rice is barely tender, 15 to 20 minutes. Drain into a sieve and rinse under cold running water. Place in a large bowl.

2. In a large skillet, melt the butter over medium-high heat. Add the ham, onion, celery, bell pepper, scallions, and garlic. Cook, stirring occasionally, until the onion is golden, 10 to 12 minutes. Add the Cajun seasoning and stir for 30 seconds.

3. Stir in the tomato sauce, 1 cup broth, the Worcestershire sauce, salt, and pepper. Bring to a simmer. Reduce the heat to medium and cook, stirring occasionally, until slightly thickened, about 10 minutes. Stir the sauce into the bowl of rice. Add the oysters and stir gently to mix. Use as a stuffing. Or place in a lightly buttered casserole, drizzle with ½ cup broth, cover, and bake as a side dish.

Paella Shrimp and Rice Stuffing

Makes about 12 cups

Rice, shrimp, and pork, golden with saffron, form the base for the classic Spanish dish, and here they become a most savory stuffing for turkey.

¼ teaspoon crushed saffron threads

½ cup dry white wine

2½ cups (1 pound) converted white rice

¼ cup olive oil

½ pound chorizo or pepperoni, cut into ½-inch cubes

1 large onion, chopped

1 large red bell pepper, chopped

1 (10-ounce) package frozen artichoke hearts, thawed and coarsely chopped

1 pound large shrimp, peeled, deveined, and cut into ½-inch pieces

1 cup pitted Spanish green olives, coarsely chopped

2 teaspoons dried oregano

2 garlic cloves, minced

⅓ cup chopped fresh parsley

1 teaspoon salt

½ teaspoon freshly ground pepper

½ cup turkey or chicken broth, optional

1. In a small bowl, stir the saffron into the wine and set aside. Bring a large pot of lightly salted water to a boil over high heat. Add the rice and reduce the heat to medium. Boil until the rice is barely tender, 15 to 20 minutes. Drain into a sieve and rinse under cold running water. Place the rice in a large bowl.

2. In a large skillet, heat the oil over medium heat. Add the chorizo and cook, stirring often, until lightly browned, about 5 minutes. Using a slotted spoon, transfer to a plate and set aside, leaving the fat in the skillet.

3. Add the onion, red pepper, and artichoke hearts to the skillet. Cook, stirring often, until the onion is softened and translucent, about 5 minutes. Stir in the shrimp, olives, oregano, and garlic. Cook, stirring often, until the shrimp just turn pink, about 3 minutes. Stir in the saffron-infused wine and bring to a boil.

4. Add the shrimp mixture with all the liquid to the rice, stirring well so the rice is evenly tinted yellow by the saffron. Add the chorizo and parsley. Season with the salt and pepper. Use as a stuffing. Or place in a lightly buttered casserole, drizzle with the broth, cover, and bake as a side dish.

Brown Rice, Basil, and Gruyère Garden Stuffing

Makes about 12 cups

When I served this colorful stuffing to guests, they gave it the ultimate stuffing compliment: it's so good, it could be served as a main course! It's equally good inside turkey or chicken.

2½ cups (1 pound) long-grain brown rice

4 tablespoons unsalted butter

1 large onion, chopped

2 medium zucchini, halved lengthwise and cut into ½-inch-thick slices

2 medium carrots, sliced ¼ inch thick

2 medium celery ribs, sliced ¼ inch thick

1 medium red bell pepper, chopped

½ pound fresh mushrooms, sliced

2 garlic cloves, minced

2 cups shredded Gruyère or Swiss cheese

½ cup chopped fresh basil

1½ teaspoons salt

½ teaspoon freshly ground pepper

½ cup turkey or chicken broth, optional

1. Bring a large pot of lightly salted water to a boil over high heat. Add the brown rice and reduce the heat to medium. Boil uncovered until the rice is barely tender, about 35 minutes. Drain into a sieve and rinse under cold running water. Place in a large bowl.

2. In a large skillet, melt the butter over medium heat. Add the onion, zucchini, carrots, celery, red pepper, mushrooms, and garlic. Cover partially and cook, stirring often, until the onion is softened and translucent and the vegetables are barely tender, 10 to 12 minutes.

3. Scrape the vegetables into the bowl of brown rice and mix well. Stir in the cheese and basil. Season with the salt and pepper. Use as a stuffing. Or place in a lightly buttered casserole, drizzle with the broth, cover, and bake as a side dish.

Five-Rice Stuffing with Baby Onions and Currants

Makes about 10 cups

Rice comes in a rainbow of hues, and they are often packaged together in colorful blends of five, or even seven, varieties, including brown, red, and black rice. (It is the hull that is colored, not the inner grain.) This is a very elegant stuffing, enhanced with glazed pearl onions and sweet currants, good with turkey or duck.

2½ cups (1 pound) five-rice blend, available at natural food and specialty
   food stores
2 tablespoons unsalted butter
3 celery ribs with leaves, chopped
1 (1-pound) bag frozen small white onions, rinsed under cold water to separate
2 to 2½ cups turkey or chicken broth, as needed
1½ cups dried currants
1 cup walnuts, toasted (page 6) and coarsely chopped
⅓ cup chopped fresh parsley
1½ teaspoons dried thyme leaves
1½ teaspoons salt
½ teaspoon freshly ground pepper

1. Bring a large pot of lightly salted water to a boil over high heat. Add the rice blend and reduce the heat to medium. Boil uncovered until the rice is barely tender, about 35 minutes. Drain into a sieve and rinse under cold running water. Place in a large bowl.

2. In a large skillet, melt the butter over medium heat. Add the celery and cook until softened, about 2 minutes. Add the onions and 2 cups broth. Bring to a boil. Cook, stirring often so the onions cook evenly, until the broth has evaporated and the onions are golden brown and glazed, 10 to 15 minutes.

3. Scrape the glazed vegetables into the bowl with the rice. Stir in the currants, walnuts, parsley, and thyme. Season with the salt and pepper. Use as a stuffing. Or place in a lightly buttered casserole, drizzle with ½ cup broth, cover, and bake as a side dish.

Wild Rice, Mushroom, and Hazelnut Stuffing

Makes about 10 cups

Wild rice is not really a true rice at all, but a grass, and the most prized versions are hand-harvested from canoes. Less expensive versions are machine-harvested, and take less time to cook. Dried cherries balance the rich flavors of the rice, wild mushrooms, and hazelnuts, to yield a versatile stuffing, fine with turkey, duck, or pork.

¾ cup dried cherries or dried cranberries

⅔ cup tawny or ruby port

3 cups (1 pound) wild rice, well rinsed

4 tablespoons unsalted butter

3 medium leeks (white parts only), cleaned and sliced

1 pound mixed wild mushrooms (such as cremini, shiitakes, and chanterelles), sliced

1 tablespoon poultry seasoning, preferably homemade (page 6)

1 cup hazelnuts, toasted and skinned (page 6), and chopped

¼ cup chopped fresh parsley

1½ teaspoons salt

½ teaspoon freshly ground pepper

½ cup turkey or chicken broth, optional

1. Place the dried cherries in a small bowl and add the port wine. Let stand while making the stuffing.

2. Bring a large pot of lightly salted water to a boil over high heat. Add the wild rice and reduce the heat to medium. Boil uncovered until the rice is barely tender (some of the rice grains may have burst), about 45 minutes. Drain the rice into a sieve and rinse under cold running water until cooled; drain well. Place in a large bowl.

3. In a very large skillet or flameproof casserole, melt 2 tablespoons of the butter over medium heat. Add the leeks and cook, stirring often, until they are tender, about 5 minutes. Add to the wild rice.

4. In the same skillet, melt the remaining 2 tablespoons butter. Add the mushrooms and cook over medium-high heat, stirring occasionally, until the mushrooms give off their juices, about 5 minutes. Add the port with cherries and the poultry seasoning and boil until the liquid is reduced to about ½ cup, 6 to 8 minutes.

5. Stir the mushrooms and port into the bowl of wild rice. Add the hazelnuts, parsley, salt, and pepper and mix well. Use as a stuffing. Or place in a lightly buttered casserole, drizzle with the broth, cover, and bake as a side dish.

Kasha, Portobello Mushroom, and Bow Tie Pasta Stuffing

You don't have to be Jewish to love kasha varnishkes, *a warming dish of buckwheat groats and bow tie pasta. This version, which also makes a great stuffing for turkey, capon, or chicken, gets a touch of sophistication from portobello mushrooms.*

½ pound bow tie pasta

1 egg

1½ cups kasha (buckwheat groats)

6 tablespoons unsalted butter or rendered chicken fat

3 to 3½ cups turkey or chicken broth, as needed

1 teaspoon salt

2 medium onions, chopped

3 medium celery ribs with leaves, chopped

2 teaspoons poultry seasoning, preferably homemade (page 6)

1 pound portobello mushrooms, trimmed (keep stems attached), halved
 lengthwise, and cut into ⅜-inch-thick slices

¼ teaspoon freshly ground pepper

I. In a large pot of boiling salted water, cook the bow ties until they are al dente, tender but still firm, 9 to 10 minutes. Drain into a colander and rinse briefly under cold running water; drain well.

2. Beat the egg lightly in a medium bowl. Add the kasha and stir until completely coated with egg. In a large skillet, melt 2 tablespoons of the butter over medium heat. Add the kasha mixture and cook, stirring often, until the egg coating is set and the kasha grains are mostly separated, about 3 minutes.

3. Add 3 cups of the broth and ½ teaspoon of the salt. Bring to a simmer; reduce the heat to low. Cover and cook until the kasha is tender and has absorbed most of the broth, about 10 minutes. Remove from the heat and let stand for 5 minutes. Transfer the kasha to a large bowl; fluff it with a fork.

4. In a large skillet, melt 2 tablespoons of the butter over medium heat. Add the onions and celery. Cook, stirring often, until the onions are golden brown, 8 to 10 minutes. Stir in the poultry seasoning. Scrape into the bowl with the kasha.

5. In the same skillet, heat the remaining 2 tablespoons of butter over medium-high heat. Add the mushrooms and cook, stirring occasionally, until the mushrooms have given off their juices, they evaporate, and the mushrooms begin to brown, about 8 minutes.

6. Add the sautéed mushrooms and cooked pasta to the kasha. Stir gently to mix. Season with the pepper and remaining ½ teaspoon salt. Use as a stuffing. Or place in a lightly buttered casserole, drizzle with ½ cup broth, cover, and bake as a side dish.

Barley and Mushroom Stuffing: Delete the kasha, egg, and 2 tablespoons butter in Step 1 and the bow tie pasta. Cook 2½ cups pearl barley in a large pot of lightly salted boiling water over medium heat until just tender, about 40 minutes. Drain well and mix with the cooked onions, celery, and mushrooms.

Polenta, Prosciutto, and Porcini Stuffing

Makes about 8 cups

Three distinctly Italian flavors merge here to create a sensational stuffing for turkey or chicken that can double as a side dish for pork. The polenta isn't soft; it's made ahead, cooled until firm, and then cut into golden yellow cubes, which make this a very special stuffing, indeed.

1½ teaspoons salt

2 cups yellow cornmeal, preferably stone-ground

1 ounce (1 cup) dried porcini mushrooms or imported Polish mushrooms

2 tablespoons olive oil

¾ pound mixed wild mushrooms (such as cremini, stemmed shiitakes, or chanterelles), trimmed and sliced

4 ounces thickly sliced prosciutto, cut into ¼-inch dice

6 scallions, chopped

1½ teaspoons dried rosemary

1½ teaspoons crumbled dried sage

2 garlic cloves, minced

¼ teaspoon freshly ground pepper

½ pound Italian or French bread, cut into ½-inch cubes and dried overnight or in the oven (about 5 cups)

¼ cup chopped fresh parsley

1 to 1½ cups turkey or chicken broth, as needed

I. Lightly oil a rimmed baking sheet. In a medium, heavy-bottomed saucepan, bring 4 cups water and 1 teaspoon of the salt to a boil over high heat. Whisking constantly, gradually add the cornmeal. Reduce the heat to low and simmer, stirring often with a wooden spatula, until the polenta is very thick and smooth, about 2 minutes. (The polenta will finish cooking when the stuffing is baked.) Pour out onto the prepared baking sheet. Using an oiled metal spatula, spread the hot polenta in a slab about ½ inch thick. Let cool completely until firm, about 45 minutes. Cut the cooled polenta into 1-inch squares. (The polenta squares can be prepared up to 1 day ahead, covered, and refrigerated.)

2. Place the dried mushrooms in a small heatproof bowl and cover with 1 cup boiling water; let stand until softened, 15 to 30 minutes. Lift out the mushrooms and chop them. Strain the soaking liquid through a wire sieve lined with a damp paper towel and reserve the liquid.

3. In a large skillet, heat the oil over medium heat. Add the fresh mushrooms, prosciutto, scallions, rosemary, sage, garlic, pepper, and remaining ½ teaspoon salt. Cook, stirring often, until the mushrooms give off their juices, about 5 minutes. Add the soaked mushrooms and the reserved soaking liquid and bring to a boil. Cook, stirring occasionally, until the mushrooms are tender and about ½ cup of liquid remains, 8 to 10 minutes.

4. Scrape the mushrooms into a large bowl. Stir in the bread cubes, polenta, and parsley. Gradually stir in about 1 cup broth, until the stuffing is evenly moistened but not soggy. Use as a stuffing. Or place in a lightly buttered casserole, drizzle with ½ cup broth, cover, and bake as a side dish.

Wild Rice and Sausage Stuffing

Makes about 10 cups

This is a classic wild rice stuffing: firm, chewy wild rice mixed with succulent sausage and crunchy toasted almonds. It's particularly good with turkey or duck.

3 cups (1 pound) wild rice, well rinsed

4 tablespoons unsalted butter

1 large onion, chopped

3 medium celery ribs with leaves, chopped

2 Granny Smith apples, peeled, cored, and chopped

1 pound bulk pork breakfast sausage

2 cups slivered almonds, toasted (page 6) and coarsely chopped

⅓ cup chopped fresh parsley

2 teaspoons poultry seasoning, preferably homemade (page 6)

¾ teaspoon salt

¼ teaspoon freshly ground pepper

½ cup turkey or chicken broth, optional

1. Bring a large pot of lightly salted water to a boil over high heat. Add the wild rice and reduce the heat to medium. Boil uncovered until the rice is barely tender, 45 to 55 minutes. Drain into a sieve and rinse under cold running water. Place in a large bowl.

2. In a large skillet, melt 2 tablespoons of the butter over medium heat. Add the onion, celery, and apples. Cook, stirring occasionally, until the onion is softened and translucent, about 6 minutes. Scrape into the bowl of rice.

3. In the same skillet, melt the remaining 2 tablespoons of butter over medium-high heat. Add the sausage and cook, stirring often and breaking up the sausage with the side of a spoon, until the meat is cooked through, about 10 minutes. Stir into the rice. Add the almonds, parsley, poultry seasoning, salt, and pepper. Mix well. Use as a stuffing. Or place in a lightly buttered casserole, drizzle with the broth, cover, and bake as a side dish.

Fruit and Vegetable
Stuffings

These stuffings highlight the flavors of fruits and vegetables. If meat makes an appearance at all, it plays a subtle, background role. Some of them are sweet with dried fruits, such as dates, prunes, and cranberries; others are savory with chiles and roasted garlic. A few don't have any bread or grain at all—just delicious fruits and vegetables cooked inside of the bird.

Potatoes show up in many of these stuffings. Use firm, waxy boiling potatoes, not mealy baking potatoes, such as russets, which will fall apart when cooked. Thin-skinned red potatoes are a good choice, as are the yellow-fleshed Yukon Gold variety. Scrub the potatoes well under cold running water. Don't bother to peel them; the skins are very tasty. Place the whole potatoes in a large saucepan and add enough lightly salted cold water to cover by two inches. Bring to a boil over high heat and cook until tender when pierced with the tip of a sharp knife. Drain, then rinse the potatoes under cold water until cool enough to handle. Cube the potatoes, but leave the skins on to help the cubes hold their shape.

Dried fruits have more intense flavors, usually hold up better than their fresh counterparts during long cooking, and add texture and color. All of the other dried fruits in this book are readily available in supermarkets, specialty food shops, and natural food stores. Supermarket varieties, which are bright and tender, have usually been treated with sulfur dioxide. The organic varieties are firmer and not very colorful, but you can use them, if you prefer.

Chestnut Stuffing with Apples and Sage

Makes about 4 cups

A *wonderful symbiotic relationship occurs between this apple-and-chestnut stuffing and the turkey. Chestnuts are very rich, so this stuffing is meant to be served in small portions—just a spoonful will do. It does not lend itself to being cooked separately as a side dish, so save it for small turkeys under 12 pounds, roasting chickens, or pork.*

3 tablespoons unsalted butter

1 large onion, chopped

½ cup semi-dry white wine, such as Riesling

3 pounds chestnuts, roasted and peeled (page 6)

2 Granny Smith or Golden Delicious apples, peeled, cored, and cut into
     ¾-inch cubes

1 tablespoon chopped fresh sage or 1½ teaspoons crumbled dried

Salt and freshly ground pepper

1. In a large skillet, melt the butter over medium heat. Add the onion and cook, stirring occasionally, until the onion is golden brown, 8 to 10 minutes.

2. Add the wine and cook until it evaporates. Stir in the roasted chestnuts, diced apples, and sage. Season with salt and pepper to taste. Use as a stuffing.

Fig, Hazelnut, and Prosciutto Stuffing

Makes about 10 cups

Modeled *after a Renaissance recipe, this interesting stuffing for turkey, chicken, or pork contrasts the sweetness of dried fruit with the saltiness of Italian ham. It is at its best with fresh rosemary, which provides a bold accent.*

4 tablespoons unsalted butter

8 ounces thick-sliced prosciutto, cut into ¼-inch cubes

1 cup chopped shallots or white parts of scallions

¾ pound soft Italian bread, cut into ½-inch cubes and dried overnight or in the oven (about 8 cups)

8 ounces dried figs, chopped (about 2 cups)

1 cup hazelnuts, toasted (page 6) and coarsely chopped

¼ cup chopped fresh parsley

1 tablespoon chopped fresh rosemary or 1½ teaspoons dried

1 to 1½ cups turkey or chicken broth, as needed

Salt and freshly ground pepper

1. In a large skillet, melt the butter over medium heat. Add the prosciutto and shallots. Cook, uncovered, stirring often, until the shallots are soft, 3 to 4 minutes.

2. Scrape the prosciutto mixture into a large bowl. Add the bread cubes, figs, hazelnuts, parsley, and rosemary. Gradually stir in about 1 cup broth, until the stuffing is evenly moistened but not soggy. Season with salt and pepper to taste. Use as a stuffing. Or place in a lightly buttered casserole, drizzle with ½ cup broth, cover, and bake as a side dish.

Chile, Hominy, and Rice Stuffing

Makes about 10 cups

Hominy is a kind of processed large-kernel corn that yields mild, chewy kernels, which are popular in Mexican and southwestern American cooking. Here it is combined with rice, cheese, and chiles for a stuffing that will add kick to the holiday bird or make a substantial meatless filling for bell peppers.

2 tablespoons olive oil

1 medium onion, chopped

1 medium green bell pepper, chopped

2 (4½-ounce) cans chopped mild green chiles, rinsed and drained

1 or 2 fresh jalapeño peppers, seeded and minced

2 garlic cloves, minced

1 tablespoon ground cumin

1 tablespoon dried oregano

1 to 1½ cups turkey or chicken broth, as needed

2½ cups (1 pound) converted white rice

2 cups shredded Monterey Jack cheese

2 (15-ounce) cans yellow or white hominy, drained and rinsed

½ cup chopped fresh cilantro

Salt and freshly ground pepper

1. In a large skillet, heat the oil over medium heat. Add the onion, bell pepper, green chiles, jalapeño pepper, and garlic. Cover and cook, stirring occasionally, until the onion and bell pepper are very soft, 6 to 8 minutes. Add the cumin and oregano and stir for 1 minute. Add 1 cup of the broth and boil until the liquid is reduced to about ¼ cup. Remove from the heat.

2. Meanwhile, bring a large pot of lightly salted water to a boil over high heat. Add the rice and reduce the heat to medium. Boil until the rice is barely tender, about 15 to 20 minutes. Drain, rinse briefly under hot running water, and drain well.

3. Transfer the hot rice to a large bowl. Add the chile mixture and the cheese, mixing until the cheese melts. Stir in the hominy and cilantro. Season with salt and pepper to taste. Use as a stuffing for turkey. Or place in a lightly buttered casserole, drizzle with ½ cup broth, cover, and bake as a side dish.

Pilaf Stuffing with Dates and Pistachios

Makes about 10 cups

Studded with sweet dates and green pistachios, this stuffing celebrates the flavors of Turkey (the country) as well as being an excellent match for turkey (the bird). Shelled, skinned pistachios are available at Indian and Middle Eastern markets and in some supermarkets; or see the note below for instructions on preparing them from unskinned nuts.

2½ cups (1 pound) basmati or Texmati rice

5 to 5½ cups turkey or chicken broth, as needed

1 teaspoon salt

4 tablespoons unsalted butter

6 scallions, chopped

¾ cup chopped dates

¾ cup chopped toasted pistachio nuts (see Note)

1 teaspoon ground cumin

½ teaspoon dried oregano

¼ teaspoon ground cinnamon

¼ teaspoon freshly ground pepper

⅓ cup chopped fresh parsley

1. In a large saucepan, bring the rice, 5 cups broth, and the salt to a boil over high heat. Reduce the heat to low and cover. Simmer until the rice is tender and the liquid is absorbed, about 15 minutes. Remove from the heat and let stand for 5 minutes. Transfer to a large bowl.

2. In a medium skillet, melt the butter over medium heat. Add the scallions. Cook, stirring often, until they are softened, 2 to 3 minutes. Add the dates, pistachios, cumin, oregano, cinnamon, and pepper. Stir until very fragrant, about 30 seconds.

3. Stir the scallion mixture and parsley into the rice. Season with additional salt to taste. Use as a stuffing. Or place in a lightly buttered casserole, drizzle with ½ cup broth, cover, and bake as a side dish.

Note: To peel pistachio nuts, drop shelled pistachios into a saucepan of boiling water for 30 seconds to loosen the skins. Drain and rinse under cold water. Pinch the nuts out of their skins. Toast as described on page 6. Let cool completely, then chop coarsely.

Smashed Potato Stuffing
with Roasted Garlic

Makes about 12 cups

Smashed potatoes are chunky, not smooth like mashed potatoes. They hold up beautifully when baked inside of a turkey or chicken. This also makes a perfect accompaniment to roast pork.

2 heads of plump, firm garlic, separated into about 40 large cloves, skins
      left on
2 tablespoons olive oil
2 tablespoons unsalted butter
8 scallions, chopped
5 pounds red or yellow potatoes, scrubbed and cut into 1½-inch chunks
1 cup sour cream
Salt and freshly ground pepper
½ cup turkey or chicken broth, optional

1. Preheat the oven to 375°F. Place the garlic on a square of aluminum foil. Drizzle with the oil and mix with your hands to coat. Fold the foil over the garlic to make a packet. Bake until the garlic is tender, about 30 minutes. Let cool, then peel, keeping the cloves as whole as possible. Set the garlic aside.

2. Meanwhile, in a medium skillet, melt the butter over medium heat. Add the scallions and cook, stirring occasionally, until softened, 2 to 3 minutes. Set the scallions aside.

3. Place the potatoes in a large saucepan and add enough cold salted water to cover. Bring to a boil over high heat. Reduce the heat to medium and cook until the potatoes are tender, 15 to 20 minutes. Drain well. Return the potatoes to the pot and place over medium heat. Stir constantly to dry out the potatoes slightly, about 2 minutes.

4. Remove from the heat. Add the sour cream, roasted garlic, and scallions to the potatoes and coarsely smash with a potato masher or a large slotted metal spoon, mixing in the sour cream. Season with salt and pepper to taste. Use as a stuffing. Or place in a lightly buttered casserole, drizzle with the broth, cover, and bake as a side dish.

Sweet Potato, Orange, and Dried Cranberry Stuffing

Makes about 7 cups

Even though dark orange-colored sweet potatoes are sometimes called "yams," they really are a sweet potato somewhat more sugary than the pale yellow variety. No matter what you call them, sweet potatoes are a holiday tradition right up there with turkey. Cranberries, too, are old pals of sweet potatoes, having shared billions of Thanksgiving meals together. While fresh cranberries are too tart to be used without being cooked first in sugar (see page 36), dried cranberries have already been lightly sweetened with corn syrup. Try this stuffing inside a turkey, heaped into the center of a crown roast of pork, or as a side dish with baked ham.

2 large yams (1½ pounds), scrubbed but not peeled

5 cups coarsely crumbled Old-Fashioned Cornbread (page 32), dried
   overnight or in the oven, or packaged cornbread stuffing

1 (11-ounce) can mandarin oranges in syrup, drained

½ cup dried cranberries

3 tablespoons chopped fresh parsley

Grated zest of 2 oranges

2 teaspoons crumbled dried sage

2 eggs, beaten

1 to 1½ cups turkey or chicken broth, as needed

½ teaspoon salt

¼ teaspoon freshly ground pepper

1. Place the yams in a large saucepan and add enough cold water to cover by 2 inches. Bring to a boil over high heat. Reduce the heat to medium and cook until the yams are just tender when pierced with the tip of a sharp knife, 20 to

25 minutes. Drain and rinse under cold water until easy to handle. Peel the yams and cut into ¾-inch cubes.

2. In a large bowl, combine the yams, cornbread, mandarin oranges, dried cranberries, parsley, orange zest, and sage. Gradually stir in the eggs and about 1 cup broth. Season with the salt and pepper. Use as a stuffing. Or place in a lightly buttered casserole, drizzle with ½ cup broth, cover, and bake as a side dish.

Passover Carrot Tsimmes Stuffing

A *beautiful stuffed capon or turkey is an excellent choice for a large Passover seder, but religious laws state that leavened bread cannot be consumed during this holiday period. Here a roasted vegetable stuffing emulates the flavors of the traditional carrot tsimmes. Plan on serving about ½ cup of this breadless stuffing per person.*

1½ pounds (1-inch diameter) small white boiling onions

1 pound medium carrots, cut into 1-inch lengths

3 tablespoons olive oil

¼ teaspoon salt

¼ teaspoon freshly ground pepper

1 cup coarsely chopped pitted dried prunes

1 cup golden raisins

1 cup walnuts, toasted (page 6) and coarsely chopped

½ teaspoon ground cinnamon

1. Preheat the oven to 400°F. To peel the onions, drop into a large saucepan of boiling water for about 30 seconds. Drain and rinse briefly under cold running water. Using a small sharp knife, cut off the root end and tip; the outer skin should slip off easily. Cut a tiny "X" in the root ends of the onions to keep them from bursting as they cook.

2. Place the peeled onions and the carrots in a large roasting pan. Drizzle on the oil and toss with your hands to coat the vegetables. Season with the salt and pepper. Roast, stirring the vegetables often, until they are tender and nicely browned, 35 to 45 minutes.

3. Transfer the vegetables to a bowl. Add the prunes, raisins, walnuts, and cinnamon and mix well. Use as a stuffing.

Artichoke, Feta Cheese, and Olive Stuffing

Makes about 3 cups

Spread this onto a butterflied leg of lamb, then roll, tie, and roast for a spectacular Easter main course. The ingredients should be chopped fairly fine so the stuffing won't fall apart when the lamb is sliced.

2 tablespoons olive oil

1 medium onion, finely chopped

1 (10-ounce) package frozen artichoke hearts, thawed and chopped

2 garlic cloves, minced

½ cup fresh bread crumbs, made from day-old Italian bread

½ cup finely crumbled feta cheese

½ cup chopped pitted black Mediterranean olives

1 egg, beaten

¼ teaspoon freshly ground black pepper

1. In a large skillet, heat the oil over medium heat. Add the onion. Cook, uncovered, stirring often, until softened, about 3 minutes. Add the artichokes and garlic and continue cooking until the onions are starting to color, about 3 more minutes. Transfer to a bowl and let cool.

2. Stir in the bread crumbs, cheese, olives, egg, and pepper. Use as stuffing for boneless leg of lamb.

Stuffed Leg of Lamb: Preheat the oven to 450°F. Place a 5-pound butterflied boneless leg of lamb, smooth-side down, on a flat work surface. Spread the stuffing over the meat, leaving a 1-inch border around the sides. Starting at a short end, roll up the roast and tie with kitchen string. Brush with 1 tablespoon olive oil and season with salt and pepper. Place on a rack in a large roasting pan. Roast 10 minutes. Reduce the oven temperature to 350°F. and continue roasting until a meat thermometer inserted in the center of the roast reads 130 to 135°F. for medium-rare, about 2 hours. Let stand 10 minutes before removing the string and carving.

Spinach, Goat Cheese, and Pine Nut Stuffing

Tuck *this tangy Mediterranean stuffing inside a boneless leg of lamb or under the skin of large chicken breasts.*

¼ cup pine nuts

2 tablespoons olive oil

1 medium onion, chopped

2 garlic cloves, minced

2 (10-ounce) packages frozen chopped spinach, thawed and squeezed to
   remove excess moisture

½ cup dried unseasoned bread crumbs

2 eggs, beaten

1 teaspoon dried rosemary

½ teaspoon dried thyme

½ teaspoon dried basil

½ teaspoon salt

¼ teaspoon freshly ground pepper

5 ounces mild white goat cheese, crumbled

1. In a medium skillet, toast the pine nuts over medium heat, stirring almost constantly, until they are lightly browned, 2 to 3 minutes. Immediately transfer to a plate to cool.

2. Add the oil to the skillet and set over medium heat. Add the onion. Cook, stirring often, until the onion is softened and just beginning to color, about 5 minutes. Add the garlic and cook for 1 minute longer. Scrape into a large bowl.

3. Add the spinach, bread crumbs, pine nuts, eggs, rosemary, thyme, and basil to the onion and garlic. Season with the salt and pepper. Fold in the crumbled goat cheese. Use as a stuffing for boned and butterflied leg of lamb (see page 81 for cooking instructions).

Meat
Stuffings

Meat stuffings add a rich component to the holiday meal. All of the stuffings in this chapter use meat as the main ingredient, with just enough bread cubes, bread crumbs, potatoes, or rice to stretch them into a generous number of servings.

One word of advice about the sliced cured meats (such as salami, mortadella, or prosciutto) in the recipes throughout the book. Your delicatessen counter is probably used to slicing these meats paper thin, especially prosciutto. Instruct the person behind the counter to slice these meats ¼ inch thick for cooking, not for sandwiches. Then they can be diced easily at home. If these meats are too thinly sliced, they will lose their character and flavor in the stuffing.

Caribbean Beef and Rice Stuffing

Makes about 10 cups

Some version of this delicious stuffing is found throughout the Caribbean and many South American countries. It works well not only as a poultry stuffing, but as a filling in vegetables like zucchini, sweet peppers, tomatoes, and pumpkin.

½ cup raisins
½ cup medium-dry sherry, such as oloroso
1½ cups converted white rice
2 tablespoons olive oil
1 large onion, chopped
1 medium red bell pepper, chopped
2 garlic cloves, minced
2 pounds ground round (85% lean)
1 cup sliced pimiento-stuffed green olives
2 teaspoons salt
½ teaspoon freshly ground pepper
2 hard-boiled eggs, coarsely chopped
1 cup slivered blanched almonds, toasted (page 6) and coarsely chopped
⅓ cup chopped fresh cilantro or parsley
½ cup turkey or chicken broth, optional

1. In a small bowl, combine the raisins and sherry. Let stand while preparing the rest of the stuffing.

2. Bring a large pot of lightly salted water to a boil over high heat. Add the rice and reduce the heat to medium. Boil uncovered until the rice is barely tender, 15 to 20 minutes. Drain into a sieve and rinse under cold running water. Place in a large bowl.

3. In a large skillet, heat the oil over medium heat. Add the onion, red pepper, and garlic. Cook, stirring occasionally, until the onion is softened, about 3 minutes. Add the ground round, olives, 1½ teaspoons of the salt, and ¼ teaspoon of the pepper. Increase the heat to medium-high. Cook, stirring often and breaking up the meat with a spoon, until the meat is no longer pink, about 10 minutes. Stir in the raisins with their sherry and bring to a boil.

4. Scrape the meat mixture into the rice. Mix in the chopped eggs, almonds, and cilantro. Season with the remaining ½ teaspoon salt and ¼ teaspoon pepper. Use as a stuffing. Or place in a lightly buttered casserole, drizzle with the broth, cover, and bake as a side dish.

Chicken Liver, Mushroom, and Brioche Stuffing with Madeira Wine

A *New York newspaper once interviewed a number of turkey experts, including myself, and we all shared our favorite ways of cooking the bird. This stuffing for turkey or chicken is a much simplified version of the one contributed by Daniel Boulud, the esteemed owner of Restaurant Daniel in Manhattan: he used foie gras; I substitute chicken livers. The French like their stuffings rich, rich, rich—and this one is no exception. If you have a French bakery nearby, purchase a buttery brioche loaf. Challah, or any other rich egg bread, can easily be substituted. If the challah comes with a poppy seed topping on the crust, just trim it off.*

4 tablespoons unsalted butter

¾ pound fresh mushrooms, sliced

1 pound chicken livers, trimmed and patted dry with paper towels

½ cup chopped shallots

½ teaspoon dried thyme leaves

½ teaspoon crumbled dried sage

Pinch of ground allspice

2 teaspoons salt

¾ teaspoon freshly ground pepper

½ cup Madeira wine

1 pound brioche or challah bread, cut into ½-inch cubes, dried overnight or in the oven (about 10 cups)

1½ cups seedless green grapes

1 cup slivered blanched almonds, toasted (page 6) and coarsely chopped

⅓ cup chopped fresh parsley

¾ to 1¼ cups turkey or chicken broth, as needed

¾ cup heavy cream

1. In a large skillet, melt 2 tablespoons of butter over medium-high heat. Add the mushrooms. Cook, stirring occasionally, until the mushrooms give off their liquid, it evaporates, and the mushrooms begin to brown, 6 to 8 minutes. Transfer to a large bowl.

2. In the same skillet, melt the remaining 2 tablespoons of butter over medium-high heat. Add the chicken livers and sauté, turning once or twice, until browned, about 3 minutes. Add the shallots, thyme, sage, allspice, ½ teaspoon of the salt, and ¼ teaspoon of the pepper. Cook, turning occasionally, until the juices evaporate and the chicken livers are cooked through with no trace of pink in the center, about 5 minutes. Add the Madeira and bring to a boil. Using a slotted spoon, transfer the livers to a cutting board. Let cool slightly, then chop into ½-inch pieces.

3. Scrape the cooking juices in the skillet into the bowl of mushrooms. Add the brioche, chopped livers, grapes, almonds, and parsley. Gradually stir in ¾ cup of broth and the heavy cream. Season with the remaining 1½ teaspoons salt and ½ teaspoon pepper. Use as a stuffing. Or place in a lightly buttered casserole, drizzle with ½ cup broth, cover, and bake as a side dish.

Santa Fe Market Chorizo and Chile Stuffing

Makes about 12 cups

Santa Fe has a colorful farmers' market with a wide variety of ingredients, including numerous varieties of just-picked chiles and corn, which are sold right off the tailgates of the farmers' trucks. This stuffing—good in turkey or chicken, as a filling for crown roast of pork, or as a side dish with pork chops— is a celebration of the delicious edibles found there and increasingly in supermarkets across the nation.

1 pound smoked chorizo or hot Italian sausage, casings removed

2 tablespoons olive oil

1 large onion, chopped

3 celery ribs, chopped

1 medium poblano, Anaheim, or green bell pepper, seeded and chopped

1 fresh jalapeño pepper, seeded and minced

2 garlic cloves, minced

1 tablespoon unseasoned ground chiles, preferably ancho, or regular chili powder

1 tablespoon dried oregano

2 teaspoons ground cumin

10 cups crumbled Old-Fashioned Cornbread (page 32), dried overnight or in the oven, or packaged cornbread stuffing (about 1 pound)

2 cups shredded sharp Cheddar cheese

2 cups fresh or thawed frozen corn kernels

⅓ cup chopped fresh cilantro

2 eggs, beaten

1 to 1½ cups turkey or chicken broth, as needed

¾ teaspoon salt

¼ teaspoon freshly ground pepper

1. If using chorizo, cut it into ½-inch dice. In a large skillet, heat the oil over medium heat. Add the chorizo; if using Italian sausage, crumble it into the pan. Cook, uncovered, stirring occasionally, until browned, about 5 minutes for chorizo and about 10 minutes for Italian sausage. Using a slotted spoon, transfer the chorizo or sausage to a plate, leaving the fat in the skillet.

2. Add the onion, celery, poblano pepper, jalapeño pepper, and garlic to the skillet. Cook over medium heat, stirring often, until the onion is golden, 8 to 10 minutes. Add the ground chiles, oregano, and cumin and stir for 1 minute.

3. Transfer the vegetable-chile mixture to a large bowl. Mix in the cornbread, reserved chorizo, cheese, corn, and cilantro. Gradually beat in the eggs and about 1 cup broth until the stuffing is evenly moistened but not soggy. Season with the salt and pepper. Use as a stuffing. Or place in a lightly buttered casserole, drizzle with ½ cup broth, cover, and bake as a side dish.

Kielbasa, Sauerkraut, and Apple Stuffing

Makes about 9 cups

Half of this recipe would be glorious in a roast goose or a couple of ducks. As described below, you'll end up with enough hearty, rib-sticking filling for a large turkey with a German accent. Be sure to use fresh sauerkraut from the refrigerated section of the market, not canned.

6 medium red potatoes

4 tablespoons unsalted butter

1 pound smoked pork or turkey kielbasa, cut into ½-inch cubes

1 large onion, chopped

2 Granny Smith apples, peeled, cored, and chopped into ½-inch cubes

2 garlic cloves, minced

2 pounds fresh sauerkraut, drained, rinsed, and squeezed to remove
    excess moisture

½ cup dry vermouth or white wine

½ teaspoon dried thyme leaves

Salt and freshly ground pepper

½ cup turkey or chicken broth, optional

1. In a large pot of boiling salted water, cook the potatoes until they are tender but still firm, 20 to 25 minutes. Drain and rinse under cold running water. Cut the potatoes into ½-inch cubes.

2. In a large skillet, melt the butter over medium heat. Add the kielbasa. Cook, stirring often, until lightly browned, about 5 minutes. Using a slotted spoon, transfer the kielbasa to a plate, leaving the fat in the skillet.

3. Add the onion, apples, and garlic to the skillet. Cook, scraping up the browned bits on the bottom of the skillet as the onions and apples give off their juices, until the onion is softened and translucent, 5 to 7 minutes. Stir in the sauerkraut, vermouth, and thyme. Cook until the sauerkraut has absorbed the vermouth, about 2 minutes.

4. Transfer to a large bowl and stir in the cooked potatoes. Season with salt and pepper to taste, but take care with the salt—sauerkraut and kielbasa are salty. Use as a stuffing for turkey. Or place in a lightly buttered casserole, drizzle with the broth, cover, and bake as a side dish.

Greek Lamb, Rice, and Dill Stuffing

Makes about 10 cups

*I*f you can't find ground lamb, the classic Greek filling for turkey, in the meat case, ask your supermarket or butcher to grind well-trimmed boneless leg of lamb, or do it yourself at home in a food processor. The dill flavor must be pronounced when the stuffing is first mixed, as its pungency is reduced when baked. In smaller amounts, this stuffing is marvelous in bell peppers, zucchini, eggplants, cabbage rolls, and even baked tomatoes.

⅔ cup dried currants
1 cup dry white wine
⅔ cup pine nuts
2½ cups (1 pound) converted white rice
2 tablespoons olive oil
8 scallions, chopped
3 garlic cloves, minced
2 pounds lean ground lamb
1½ teaspoons salt
½ teaspoon freshly ground pepper
½ cup chopped fresh dill
½ cup turkey or chicken broth, optional

1. Place the currants in a small bowl, add the wine, and let stand while preparing the rest of the stuffing ingredients.

2. In a large skillet, toast the pine nuts over medium heat, stirring almost constantly, until lightly browned, 2 to 3 minutes. Immediately transfer to a plate to cool.

3. Bring a large pot of lightly salted water to a boil over high heat. Add the rice and reduce the heat to medium. Boil uncovered until the rice is barely tender, 15 to 20 minutes. Drain and rinse under cold running water. Place in a large bowl.

4. In a large skillet, heat the oil over medium heat. Add the scallions and garlic. Cook, uncovered, until the scallions are wilted, 2 to 3 minutes. Add the ground lamb, salt, and pepper and increase the heat to medium-high. Cook, stirring often and breaking up the meat with a spoon, until the lamb is well-done, about 10 minutes. Tilt the pan to drain off the lamb fat, which can be strong tasting. Stir in the currants with their wine, the pine nuts, and the dill. Bring to a boil and cook until the wine is reduced to about ¼ cup, about 5 minutes.

5. Stir the lamb mixture into the rice. Season with additional salt and pepper to taste. Use as a stuffing. Or place in a lightly buttered casserole, drizzle with the broth, cover, and bake as a side dish.

Mortadella, Walnut, and Rosemary Stuffing

Mortadella, a delicately flavored cured pork sausage with a mousse-like texture, is the true bologna, originating in the Italian city of the same name. It makes a good sandwich, but it is also an excellent addition to stuffing, since it adds both richness and flavor. Use this stuffing for turkey, chicken, or pork.

4 tablespoons unsalted butter

1 medium onion, chopped

2 garlic cloves, minced

4 cups fresh bread crumbs, made from day-old Italian bread (about
      7 ounces)

½ pound thick-sliced mortadella, casings removed, cut into ½-inch dice

1 cup walnuts, toasted and coarsely chopped

½ cup freshly grated Parmesan cheese

1 tablespoon chopped fresh rosemary or 1½ teaspoons dried

¼ teaspoon salt

¼ teaspoon freshly ground pepper

2 eggs, beaten

½ cup turkey or chicken broth, optional

1. In a large skillet, melt the butter over medium heat. Add the onion. Cook, uncovered, stirring often, until the onion is translucent, about 5 minutes. Add the garlic and cook for 1 minute.

2. Scrape the onion and garlic into a large bowl. Stir in the bread crumbs, mortadella, walnuts, Parmesan cheese, rosemary, salt, and pepper. Gradually stir in the eggs. Use as a stuffing. Or place in a lightly buttered casserole, drizzle with the broth, cover, and bake as a side dish.

Antipasto Stuffing with Salami and Provolone

Makes about 7 cups

A couple of boxes of Italian-seasoned salad croutons tossed with a few purchased items from the deli counter add up to an almost instant stuffing for turkey or chicken. To crush the croutons, leave them in their bags, then roll them under a rolling pin or press with a heavy skillet.

2 (5½ ounce) boxes Italian-seasoned salad croutons, coarsely crushed

¼ pound thick-sliced Genoa salami, cut into ¼-inch dice

¼ pound thick-sliced provolone cheese, cut into ¼-inch dice

1 cup black Mediterranean olives, pitted and coarsely chopped

1 (7-ounce) jar roasted vinegar-packed Italian red peppers, drained and
      chopped

2 eggs, beaten

1 to 1½ cups turkey or chicken broth, as needed

1. In a large bowl, combine the crushed croutons, salami, provolone, olives, and red peppers. Gradually stir in the eggs and about 1 cup broth, until the stuffing is evenly moistened but not soggy.

2. Let stand, stirring occasionally, about 10 minutes. Use as a stuffing. Or place in a lightly buttered casserole, drizzle with ½ cup broth, cover, and bake as a side dish

Pork, Prune, and Chestnut Stuffing

Makes about 8 cups

*S*panish inspired, this rich, meaty stuffing, bound heavily with eggs, makes a festive, seasonal filling for a very grand turkey.

¾ cup diced (½-inch) pitted prunes

½ cup tawny or ruby port

2 tablespoons olive oil

1 large onion, chopped

2 garlic cloves, minced

1½ pounds ground pork

1 teaspoon imported sweet paprika

½ teaspoon ground cinnamon

½ teaspoon ground cumin

1½ teaspoons salt

½ teaspoon freshly ground pepper

4 cups fresh bread crumbs, prepared from day-old Italian bread (about
     7 ounces)

1 pound chestnuts, roasted (page 6), peeled, and coarsely chopped

4 eggs, beaten

½ cup turkey or chicken broth, optional

1. In a small bowl, combine the prunes and port and let stand while making the stuffing.

2. In a large skillet, heat the oil over medium heat. Add the onion and cook, stirring occasionally, until softened and translucent, about 5 minutes. Add the garlic and stir for 30 seconds. Add the pork and cook, stirring often and breaking up the meat with a spoon, until cooked through, about 10 minutes. Add the paprika, cinnamon, cumin, 1 teaspoon of the salt, and ¼ teaspoon of the pepper and stir until very fragrant, about 30 seconds. Add the prunes with their port and bring to a boil.

3. Transfer the pork mixture to a large bowl. Add the bread crumbs, chestnuts, and eggs to the pork mixture and mix well. Season with the remaining ½ teaspoon salt and ¼ teaspoon pepper. Use as a stuffing. Or place in a lightly buttered casserole, drizzle with the broth, cover, and bake as a side dish.

Savory Sausage and Mushroom Stuffing

Makes about 8 cups

You have to look awfully hard to find someone who doesn't love sausage-stuffed mushroom caps...or this stuffing for turkey or stuffed vegetables, especially eggplant or mushroom caps.

¼ cup olive oil
1 medium onion, chopped
2 garlic cloves, minced
1 pound sweet Italian pork or turkey sausage, casings removed
1 teaspoon dried basil
1 teaspoon dried marjoram
¾ pound brown Italian mushrooms (cremini), sliced
10 cups fresh bread crumbs, made from day-old Italian bread (about 1 pound)
1 cup freshly grated Parmesan cheese
½ cup chopped fresh parsley
2 cups turkey or chicken broth, as needed
Salt and freshly ground pepper

1. In a large skillet, heat 2 tablespoons of the oil over medium heat. Add the onion and garlic. Cook, uncovered, stirring often, until the onion is softened, about 3 minutes. Add the sausage, basil, and marjoram. Cook, stirring often and breaking up the meat with a spoon, until the sausage is cooked through, about 10 minutes. Scrape into a large bowl.

2. Add the remaining 2 tablespoons of oil to the skillet and heat over medium heat. Add the mushrooms. Cook, uncovered, until the mushrooms give off their juices, they evaporate, and the mushrooms begin to brown, about 8 minutes.

3. Add the mushrooms to the sausage in the bowl. Mix in the bread crumbs, mushrooms, Parmesan cheese, and parsley. Gradually stir in about 1½ cups of broth. Season with salt and pepper to taste. Use as a stuffing. Or place in a lightly buttered casserole, drizzle with ½ cup broth, cover, and bake as a side dish.

Turkey Pâté Stuffing

Makes about 8 cups

Here's another turkey stuffing with meaty flavors, accented with brandy and dotted with pistachios. The French often prepare their pâtés with ground veal, but ground turkey is less expensive and easier to find.

4 tablespoons unsalted butter

1 cup chopped shallots or white parts of scallions

1½ pounds ground turkey

1½ pounds ground pork

2 teaspoons dried thyme

¼ teaspoon ground allspice

Pinch of grated nutmeg

2 teaspoons salt

½ teaspoon freshly ground pepper

¼ cup brandy

4 cups fresh bread crumbs, prepared from day-old Italian bread (about 7
     ounces)

½ chopped skinned pistachio nuts (see Note, page 75)

⅓ cup chopped fresh parsley

4 eggs, beaten

½ cup turkey or chicken broth, optional

I. In a large skillet, melt the butter over medium heat. Add the shallots and cook until softened, about 2 minutes. Add the ground turkey, ground pork, thyme, allspice, nutmeg, salt, and pepper. Increase the heat to medium-high. Cook, uncovered, stirring often with a wooden spoon to break up the meat, until the meat is cooked through, 10 to 12 minutes. Add the brandy, bring to a boil, and cook for 1 minute.

2. Scrape the meat mixture into a large bowl. Add the bread crumbs, pistachios, and parsley. Gradually stir in the eggs. Use as a stuffing. Or place in a lightly buttered casserole, drizzle with the broth, cover, and bake as a side dish.

Florentine Sausage, Ricotta, and Spinach Stuffing

Makes about 7 cups

This combination of ingredients makes a soft, spoonable, luscious turkey stuffing. Try it also in Cornish game hens, breast of veal, red bell peppers, or large zucchini.

2 tablespoons olive oil

1 large onion, chopped

2 garlic cloves, minced

1 pound sweet or hot Italian sausage, casings removed

1 tablespoon Italian seasoning blend

2 cups fresh bread crumbs, made from day-old Italian bread

1 (15-ounce) container ricotta cheese

2 (10-ounce) packages frozen chopped spinach, thawed and squeezed to
    remove excess moisture

½ cup freshly grated Parmesan cheese

2 eggs, beaten

¼ teaspoon grated nutmeg

½ teaspoon salt

¼ teaspoon freshly ground pepper

1. In a large skillet, heat the oil over medium heat. Add the onion and garlic. Cook, uncovered, stirring often, until the onion is softened, about 3 minutes. Add the sausage and Italian seasoning. Increase the heat to medium-high. Cook, stirring often and breaking up the meat with a spoon, until the sausage is cooked through, about 10 minutes.

2. Scrape the sausage mixture into a large bowl. Mix in the bread crumbs, ricotta cheese, spinach, Parmesan cheese, eggs, nutmeg, salt, and pepper. Use as a stuffing. Or place in a lightly buttered shallow baking dish, bake uncovered, and serve as a side dish.

Index

A

Almond(s)
  cornbread stuffing, gingered cranberry and, 36
  to toast, 6
Antipasto stuffing with salami and provolone, 95
Apple(s)
  chestnut stuffing with sage and, 70
  in Mason-Dixon cornbread dressing with pecans and bacon, 38
  pumpernickel and rye bread stuffing with walnuts, golden raisins, and, 30
  sausage, and sage stuffing, quick, 15
  kielbasa, and sauerkraut stuffing, 90
Apricots, aromatic basmati rice with cashews and, 50

Aromatic basmati rice with apricots and cashews, 50
Artichoke(s)
  feta cheese, and olive stuffing, 81
  sourdough bread stuffing with sun-dried tomatoes, basil, and, 20

B

Bacon
  and greens cornbread stuffing, 33
  Mason-Dixon cornbread dressing with pecans and, 38
  potato, and rye bread stuffing, 24
Barley and mushroom stuffing, 65
Basil

brown rice, and Gruyère garden stuffing, 58
  sourdough bread stuffing with artichokes, sun-dried tomatoes, and, 20
Basmati rice with apricots and cashews, aromatic, 50
Bayou eggplant and shrimp stuffing, 44
Beef and rice stuffing, Caribbean, 84
Bow tie pasta stuffing, kasha, portobello mushroom, and, 64
Bread, about, 5, 11
Bread stuffing(s), 11–30. *See also* Crackers
  giblet and, 13
  with onions, celery, and herbs, classic, 12
  oyster and, 13
  pumpernickel and rye,

with apples, walnuts,
and golden raisins, 30
raisin, ham, fennel, and,
14
rye, potato, bacon, and,
24
sausage and, 13
sourdough, with arti-
chokes, sun-dried toma-
toes, and basil, 20
whole wheat, and roasted
vegetable stuffing, 16
Brioche, chicken liver, and
mushroom stuffing with
Madeira wine, 86
Broth, turkey, 9
Brown rice, basil, and Gruyère
garden stuffing, 58

C

Cajun seasoning, homemade,
6
Caribbean beef and rice
stuffing, 84
Carrot tsimmes stuffing,
Passover, 80
Cashews, aromatic basmati
rice with apricots and,
50
Celery, classic bread stuffing
with onions, herbs, and,
12
Cheese
feta, artichoke, and olive
stuffing, 81

goat, spinach, and pine
nut stuffing, 82
Gruyère, brown rice, and
basil garden stuffing, 58
provolone, antipasto stuffing with salami and, 95
ricotta, Florentine, and
sausage stuffing, 102
Chestnut(s), 7
to roast, 6–7
stuffing
with apples and sage, 70
pork, prune, and, 96
Chicken liver, mushroom,
and brioche stuffing
with Madeira wine, 86
Chile
hominy, and rice stuffing,
72
and chorizo stuffing, Santa
Fe market, 88
Chinese hidden treasure
stuffing, 52
Chorizo and chile stuffing,
Santa Fe market, 88
Clams, Portuguese cornbread
stuffing with spicy
sausage and, 46
Classic bread stuffing with
onions, celery, and
herbs, 12
Cornbread (stuffings), 31–47
in Bayou eggplant and
shrimp stuffing, 44
with clams and spicy
sausage, Portuguese, 46

in crab gumbo stuffing, 40
dressing
with bacon and pecans,
Mason-Dixon, 38
with ham, peaches, and
peanuts, quick
Southern, 34
gingered cranberry and
almond, 36
greens and bacon, 33
old-fashioned, 32
with turkey giblets, dirty,
42
Corn chowder stuffing, New
England oyster and, 28
Crab gumbo stuffing, 40
Cracker(s)
oyster, in New England
oyster and corn chowder
stuffing, 28
saltine, in peppery sausage
and cracker stuffing, 26
Cranberry
and almond cornbread
stuffing, gingered, 36
dried, sweet potato, and
orange stuffing, 78
Currants, five-rice stuffing
with baby onions and, 60

D

Dates, pilaf stuffing with pistachios and, 74
Dill, Greek lamb, and rice
stuffing, 92

Dirty cornbread stuffing with turkey giblets, 42
Dried cranberry stuffing, sweet potato, orange, and, 78

E

Eggplant and shrimp stuffing, Bayou, 44

F

Fennel, ham, and raisin bread stuffing, 14
Feta cheese, artichoke, and olive stuffing, 81
Fig, hazelnut, and prosciutto stuffing, 71
Florentine sausage, ricotta, and spinach stuffing, 102
Fruits, dried, 69
Fruit stuffings, 69–82
    chestnut stuffing with apples and sage, 70
    fig, hazelnut, and prosciutto stuffing, 71
    pilaf stuffing with dates and pistachios, 74
    sweet potato, orange, and dried cranberry stuffing, 78

G

Garlic, roasted, smashed potato stuffing with, 76

Giblet(s)
    and bread stuffing, 13
    turkey, dirty cornbread stuffing with, 42
Gingered cranberry and almond cornbread stuffing, 36
Goat cheese, spinach, and pine nut stuffing, 82
Gravy, perfect roast turkey with, 8
Greek lamb, rice, and dill stuffing, 92
Greens and bacon cornbread stuffing, 33
Gruyère, brown rice, and basil garden stuffing, 58
Gumbo stuffing, crab, 40

H

Ham. *See also* Prosciutto
    fennel, and raisin bread stuffing, 14
    and oyster stuffing, jambalaya, 54
    quick Southern cornbread dressing with peaches, peanuts, and, 34
Hazelnut(s)
    fig, and prosciutto stuffing, 71
    to roast, 6
    wild rice, and mushroom stuffing, 62

Herbs, classic bread stuffing with onions, celery, and, 12
Hominy, chile, and rice stuffing, 72

I

Ingredients, 5–7

J

Jambalaya ham and oyster stuffing, 54

K

Kasha, portobello mushroom, and bow tie pasta stuffing, 64
Kielbasa, sauerkraut, and apple stuffing, 90

L

Lamb
    leg of, stuffed, 81
    rice, and dill stuffing, Greek, 92
Leg of lamb, stuffed, 81
Liver, chicken, mushroom, and brioche stuffing with Madeira wine, 86
Low-fat turkey sausage and vegetable stuffing, 18

M

Madeira wine, chicken liver, mushroom, and brioche stuffing with, 86
Mason-Dixon cornbread dressing with bacon and pecans, 38
Meat stuffings, 83–102
  antipasto stuffing with salami and provolone, 95
  beef and rice stuffing, Caribbean, 84
  chicken liver, mushroom, and brioche stuffing with Madeira wine, 86
  chorizo and chile stuffing, Santa Fe market, 88
  kielbasa, sauerkraut, and apple stuffing, 90
  lamb, rice, and dill stuffing, Greek, 92
  mortadella, walnut, and rosemary stuffing, 94
  pork, prune, and chestnut stuffing, 96
  sausage and mushroom stuffing, savory, 98
  sausage, ricotta, and spinach stuffing, Florentine, 102
  turkey pâté stuffing, 100
Mortadella, walnut, and rosemary stuffing, 94
Mushroom
  and barley stuffing, 65

chicken liver, and brioche stuffing with Madeira wine, 86
portobello, kasha, and bow tie pasta stuffing, 64
and sausage stuffing, savory, 98
wild rice, and hazelnut stuffing, 62

N

New England oyster and corn chowder stuffing, 28
Nut(s). *See also specific nuts*
  to roast, 6–7
  pine, spinach, and goat cheese stuffing, 82

O

Old-fashioned cornbread for stuffing, 32
Olive, artichoke, and feta cheese stuffing, 81
Onions
  baby, five-rice stuffing with currants and, 60
  classic bread stuffing with celery, herbs, and, 12
Orange, sweet potato, and dried cranberry stuffing, 78
Oyster
  and bread stuffing, 13

and jambalaya ham stuffing, 54
Oyster crackers, in New England oyster and corn chowder stuffing, 28

P

Paella shrimp and rice stuffing, 56
Passover carrot tsimmes stuffing, 80
Pasta, bow tie, stuffing, kasha, portobello mushroom, and, 64
Pâté stuffing, turkey, 100
Peaches, quick Southern cornbread dressing with ham, peanuts, and, 34
Peanuts, quick Southern cornbread dressing with ham, peaches, and, 34
Pecans
  Mason-Dixon cornbread dressing with bacon and, 38
  to roast, 6
Peppery sausage and cracker stuffing, 26
Perfect roast turkey with gravy, 8
Pilaf stuffing with dates and pistachios, 74
Pine nut stuffing, spinach, goat cheese, and, 82
Pistachios

pilaf stuffing with dates and, 74
to roast, 6
Polenta, prosciutto, and porcini stuffing, 66
Porcini, polenta, and prosciutto stuffing, 66
Pork, prune, and chestnut stuffing, 96
Portobello mushroom, kasha, and bow tie pasta stuffing, 64
Portuguese cornbread stuffing with clams and spicy sausage, 46
Potato(es), 69
  bacon, and rye bread stuffing, 24
  smashed, stuffing with roasted garlic, 76
Poultry seasoning, homemade, 6
Prosciutto
  fig, and hazelnut stuffing, 71
  polenta, and porcini stuffing, 66
Provolone, antipasto stuffing with salami and, 95
Prune, pork, and chestnut stuffing, 96
Pumpernickel and rye bread stuffing with apples, walnuts, and golden raisins, 30

Q

Quick sausage, apple, and sage stuffing, 15
Quick Southern cornbread dressing with ham, peaches, and peanuts, 34

R

Raisin(s)
  bread stuffing, ham, fennel, and, 14
  golden, pumpernickel and rye bread stuffing with apples, walnuts, and, 30
Rice stuffings, 49–68
  basmati rice with apricots and cashews, aromatic, 50
  brown rice, basil, and Gruyère garden stuffing, 58
  Caribbean beef and rice stuffing, 84
  chile, hominy, and rice stuffing, 72
  Chinese hidden treasure stuffing, 52
  five-rice stuffing with baby onions and currants, 60
  Greek lamb, rice, and dill stuffing, 92
  jambalaya ham and oyster stuffing, 54
  paella shrimp and rice stuffing, 56

Rick's deluxe turkey stuffing, 22
Ricotta, sausage, and spinach stuffing, Florentine, 102
Roasted garlic, smashed potato stuffing with, 76
Roasted vegetable stuffing, whole wheat bread and, 16
Roasting nuts, 6–7
Roast turkey with gravy, perfect, 8
Rosemary, mortadella, and walnut stuffing, 94
Rye bread stuffing
  with apples, walnuts, and golden raisins, pumpernickel and, 30
  potato, bacon, and, 24

S

Sage
  chestnut stuffing with apples and, 70
  sausage, and apple stuffing, quick, 15
Salami, antipasto stuffing with provolone and, 95
Santa Fe market chorizo and chile stuffing, 88
Sauerkraut, kielbasa, and apple stuffing, 90
Sausage
  apple, and sage stuffing, quick, 15
  bread stuffing and, 13

low-fat turkey, and veg-
etable stuffing, 18
and mushroom stuffing,
savory, 98
peppery, and cracker stuffing, 26
ricotta, and spinach stuffing, Florentine, 102
spicy, Portuguese corn-
bread stuffing with
clams and, 46
and wild rice stuffing, 68
Savory sausage and mush-
room stuffing, 98
Seasonings, about, 6
Shrimp
and rice stuffing, paella,
56
stuffing, Bayou eggplant
and, 44
Smashed potato stuffing with
roasted garlic, 76
Sourdough bread stuffing
with artichokes, sun-
dried tomatoes, and
basil, 20
Southern cornbread dressing
with ham, peaches, and
peanuts, quick, 34
Spinach

goat cheese, and pine nut
stuffing, 82
sausage, and ricotta stuffing, Florentine, 102
Stuffed leg of lamb, 81
Stuffing turkeys, 4–5
Sweet potato, orange, and
dried cranberry stuffing,
78

T

Toasting nuts, 6–7
Tomatoes, sun-dried, sourdough bread stuffing
with artichokes, basil,
and, 20
Tsimmes stuffing, Passover
carrot, 80
Turkey, 7
broth, 9
giblets, dirty cornbread
stuffing with, 42
pâté stuffing, 100
perfect roast, with gravy, 8
sausage, low-fat, and vegetable stuffing, 18
stuffing, 4–5
Turnips, in bacon and greens
cornbread stuffing, 33

V

Vegetable stuffing
low-fat turkey sausage and, 18
roasted, whole wheat
bread and, 16

W

Walnut(s)
mortadella, and rosemary
stuffing, 94
pumpernickel and rye
bread stuffing with
apples, golden raisins,
and, 30
to roast, 6
Whole wheat bread and
roasted vegetable stuff-
ing, 16
Wild rice
mushroom, and hazelnut
stuffing, 62
and sausage stuffing, 68
Wine, Madeira, chicken liver,
mushroom, and brioche
stuffing with, 86